WHAT PRICE THE LOTTERY

WHAT PRICE
THE
LOTTERY

KEITH TONDEUR

MONARCH
Crowborough

First published 1996

ISBN 1 85424 349 7

British Library Cataloguing in Publication Data
A catalogue record for this book is available
from the British Library.

Cartoons by Taffy

Production and Printing in England for
MONARCH PUBLICATIONS
Broadway House, The Broadway, Crowborough,
East Sussex TN6 1HQ by
Nuprint Ltd, Station Road, Harpenden, Herts AL5 4SE

CONTENTS

This book is dedicated to Geoff and Betty Bell
– two good and faithful servants

ACKNOWLEDGEMENTS

I am extremely grateful to a number of people for their help in writing this book. First, thanks must go to John Ashcroft of the Jubilee Centre. In January 1993 he produced a report entitled 'All in a good cause?' about the National Lottery. Reading the report three years later shows how accurate his forecasts were with all areas of concern turning out to be key issues currently under discussion. I have drawn heavily on this report in the introductory chapter. I am also grateful to Martyn Eden of Evangelical Alliance and Dave Cave for sound Christian input. Thanks too to Tina Lambert for her help with the research and Liz Lown for getting the book typed up so quickly.

This book has been written in record time so I have been even harder to live with than usual. Special thanks must go to my wife, Carole, and to Luke, John and baby Grace for putting up with me.

'The whore and gambler, by the state licensed, build the nation's fate' (William Blake, *Augaries of Innocence*).

'The Lottery, with its weekly payout of enormous prizes was the one public event to which the proles paid serious attention. It was probable that there were some millions of proles for whom the Lottery was their principal, if not the only reason, for staying alive. It was their delight, their folly, their anodyne, their intellectual stimulant. Where the Lottery was concerned even people who could barely read and write seemed capable of intricate calculations and staggering feats of memory. There was a whole tribe of men who made a living simply by selling systems forecasts and lucky amulets' (George Orwell, *1984* [written in 1949]).

'The National Lottery is harmless fun' (Mrs Bottomley, National Heritage Secretary).

'People looking back in twenty-five years' time may find that this was the release of a great evil in society. A quarter or half a million extra compulsive gamblers could mean a huge amount of misery' (Mr Fitzherbert, Directory of Social Change and author of the Rowntree Report on the National Lottery).

INTRODUCTION

I feel I should say at the outset of this book that as the director of a national money education charity and a committed Christian I have strong reservations about the National Lottery. However, I also recognise that it is seen and enjoyed by many as harmless fun as they dream of unexpected riches and everything they ever wanted.

As I write, the National Lottery has been in existence for about eighteen months. During that time a large number of people will have won nothing and a considerable number will have won small prizes. For a few, millions of pounds will have come into their possession. For a few more the National Lottery will have become an addiction that could well have serious adverse consequences. Certainly at Credit Action we are beginning to see debt problems that have gambling as their root cause. It is for this very reason that we will not apply to the National Lottery for funding as we feel it would be hypocritical to take money from something which we feel could be contributing to people's problems.

Despite personal feelings I don't think anyone could argue that the Lottery has not been successful in achieving its aims. It is highly popular and, now that payments are regularly being given to charities, some of the criticism may become more muted. However, it is likely that the debate will continue for some considerable time to come and this book has been written because I believe several issues have to be addressed. Some of the areas we will look at are:

- The effects on the 'winners' and 'losers'
- The effects on charities, the young and society in general
- A Christian perspective
- The changes which may need to be made

I hope this book will help clarify people's thinking about the National Lottery. Certainly, I believe it will raise issues that will need addressing if it is to both remain popular and also remain aware of the possible negative impact it could well be having on certain sections of our society.

CHAPTER 1

BACKGROUND TO THE LOTTERY

Raising money for good causes is obviously something that nearly everybody would applaud.

However, claims that enormous sums of money can be raised by the Lottery without there being negative pressures elsewhere would appear at face value to be too simplistic. The benefits, especially to 'good causes', can be clearly seen but can in certain circumstances be exaggerated – for example where a charity would have received a similar income by public donation. The costs can be significantly underestimated and in human terms this can be particularly true because of the hidden nature of any form of compulsive gambling.

The aim of this book is to take as even-handed an approach as possible. The Lottery is clearly not a panacea for all the problems of individuals or even society but it has rapidly become a well-known national institution. In the short time it has been in existence it has attracted enormous controversy. You raise the topic and there will be a wide divergence of views – the impact on charitable giving, whether there should be a maximum 'cap' on the jackpot payout, what it is saying about our society today.

The experience of lotteries in other countries which have been running for much longer than ours indicate degrees of both social and economic costs. The differences between these various countries and the ways in which they are structured mean that there is no clear definitive pattern and that therefore what is happening in one country will not necessarily be repeated in another. Notwithstanding this argument, however, the experience of other countries indicates that there are some potential dangers in having a lottery and these are likely to increase as time goes by.

It is vital therefore that these issues are addressed speedily before problems mount. Certainly, they should not be lightly dismissed as being irrelevant to our Lottery. If they are ignored there is a real long-term danger that as problems, and therefore criticism, mount there will be many who turn away from the Lottery – and maybe even from the charities associated with it. This could then lead to a situation where our aim to benefit 'good causes' could actually prove detrimental to them. This would prove disastrous. It is important that we look at history to ensure that these sort of mistakes are not repeated.

The History of Lotteries in Britain

The first recorded lottery to take place in England was in 1569 when money was raised primarily to help the Cinque Ports. Over the next one hundred years or so various other lotteries were promoted, nearly always for public purposes. Examples of these ranged from raising money to bring fresh water to London to helping poor and injured soldiers. All of these lotteries were completely regulated by the State – Parliament taking over control from the King in 1698. It was also in that year that Parliament decreed that in future all lotteries had to be initially authorised by Parliament because several earlier lotteries had led to scandal amidst strong allegations of corruption. By 1776 the State was running a National Lottery as an annual event, but there was ever increasing opposition to it, partly due to the whiff of corruption which surrounded it, but even more so because of the attendant social evils.

By 1807 things had got so bad that William Wilberforce and Henry Thornton, having been at long last successful in achieving the abolition of the slave trade, decided that the Lottery had to be the next thing to go. Wilberforce was to devote the last few months of his life to the campaign. However, despite a highly critical report by a Select Committee in 1808 which commented, 'In truth the foundation of the lottery is so radically vicious that your Committee feel convinced that under no system of regulations which can be devised will it be possible for Parliament to adopt it as an efficient source of revenue, and at the same time divest it of all the evils and calamities of which it has hitherto proved so baneful a source', the lotteries continued. They were eventually stopped in 1826.

Since then the State's official position on gambling and the Lottery has been mainly one of disapproval. The Royal Commission on Lotteries and Betting which took place in 1932/3 recommended a gentle relaxation of the law to allow small lotteries for charitable or philanthropic purposes. This was allowed purely on the grounds that the reason for buying a lottery ticket was to give help to others in distress rather than the hope for personal gain. On the subject of a National Lottery the Commission was dismissive:

'In the history of public finance, lotteries take their place among the expedients which are resorted to when other and more reputable methods of finance have failed. It is significant that in this country lotteries were abandoned when more assured sources of income became available to the State.'

The next Commission on Betting, Lotteries and Gambling took place between 1949 and 1951 and was certainly not as critical in its findings. It doubted whether the introduction of a National Lottery would lead to an excess of gambling and consequent problems. They argued that the major problems of the eighteenth century would not be repeated because at that time the National Lottery was sold with one of the first intensive publicity campaigns, while the population now was much more sophisticated and would not react to such pressures. [This does of course call into question the billions of pounds spent on advertising annually and more specifically the whole focus of the 'It could be you' campaign with which the National Lottery was launched.] However, the Commission came to the conclusion that a National Lottery would increase the total volume of gambling. They concluded therefore that it was, in principle, wrong for the State to encourage or even provide any sort of facility for gambling and were thus not prepared to recommend a National Lottery.

By 1978 things had changed. The Royal Commission reported by recommending the creation of a National Lottery for good causes. They argued that there was no reason for the State not to promote a gambling enterprise when it was both popular and socially harmless, and when it was also designed to raise money for good causes. It concluded that a National Lottery would fulfil all these requirements as long as it was carefully and strictly established and monitored. From then until 1992 a number of private members' bills were introduced to Parliament on the subject but because of either time pressures or lack of support none were successful.

The National Lottery Etc. Bill

In March 1992 [and very shortly before an election] the Government published a White Paper which recommended establishing a single National Lottery to raise money for good causes. The Conservative Party subsequently adopted this as part of their election manifesto in the following month. After their victory the above Bill was published in 1992 and successfully went through Parliament the following year.

At that stage tenders had to be submitted to run the Lottery and these came from a variety of sources, including Richard Branson, who offered to run it on a 'non-profit' basis. In spite of that, or perhaps even because of it, the contract was awarded to Camelot which runs the Lottery along commercial lines. Thus Camelot is a private limited company which pays dividends to its shareholders. These comprise

Cadbury Schweppes, the security printer De La Rue, the lottery equipment company G-Tech, Racal Electronics and the computer group ICL.

Naturally, Camelot has had to work within the framework for running the Lottery and distributing the profits that the Bill set out. It is under the direction of the National Heritage Secretary. Once the licence to run the National Lottery was awarded it was also able to run various other lottery-type games and has therefore been able to establish a range of different 'scratch' cards. The difference between these two types of gambling is that when you buy a Lottery ticket you select any six numbers between one and forty-nine at £1 a time or allow the machine to pick six random numbers for you. Once you have marked your card you hand it in with your money to a Camelot outlet, usually a newsagent, Post Office or garage, which has specialist equipment fitted enabling your card numbers to be recorded and passed immediately to Camelot headquarters. You need to keep your original card as it is on that that the winnings are paid out – for small prizes at a Camelot outlet or for big ones from a Camelot regional office.

'Scratch' cards are also available from these and other sources. There are two different sorts of cards. You either have to scratch off the material which covers the six amounts and if any three are the same you have won the amount stated. Alternatively if your scratch off score beats their score you win the prize shown on the card. These cards are addictive: it is the fact that many people feel they have nearly won, and therefore should try again, that has caused so much criticism.

The Bill also proposed the setting up of a National Lottery Distribution Fund which would be split into separate accounts for the five different distributing bodies. These would cover sport, the arts, national heritage, charitable expenditure and the Millennium Fund for projects which will mark the year 2000. It was decided at the beginning that each body would receive 20% of the Distribution Fund, although the National Heritage Secretary does have the power to vary these sums significantly as long as not less than 5% goes to any body. It was decided that the money would be awarded to 'good causes' selected by existing organisations such as the Arts Council, the Sports Council and the National Heritage Memorial Fund and that new bodies – the National Lotteries Charities Board and the Millennium Commission – would need to be established for distributing funds in these particular sectors. Within the sports, arts and charitable spending, provision is also made for the allocation of separate funding for England, Scotland, Wales and Northern Ireland.

In addition the Bill also gave the Heritage Secretary sweeping powers which include making regulations as to where and how lottery tickets can be bought, the minimum age at which someone can buy a ticket and what information can appear in any advertising that takes place. There were no specific details of exactly how the games should be pursued in the Bill. Camelot, therefore, has to refer to the National Heritage Secretary before doing something new. Plans to have a twice-weekly draw may well be looked on favourably in time, for example, especially as the amount of money being spent on the existing lottery shows signs of peaking. However, plans by Camelot to 'double-up' the jackpot to celebrate their first anniversary were flatly rejected. This was probably due to the fact that there are a number of indicators that an enhanced jackpot will lead to certain individuals significantly overcommitting their family budget to buy tickets. As it is, the odds of winning the jackpot in a normal week have been calculated as 1 in 14 million, although scratch cards offer a much higher chance of winning smaller, but still significant sums of money.

Finally, the Bill allowed an increase in individual prize limits to £25,000 for smaller lotteries and the restriction on the total value of tickets sold by them was raised to £250,000. Simply by comparing the National Lottery jackpot of a typical week (say £8 million) with smaller lotteries' prizes of £25,000 clearly shows why so many charitable lotteries have suffered so badly with many having to cut back or even close completely.

Lotteries in other countries

Another hidden pressure for the introduction of a British National Lottery undoubtedly came from the European Community. Every other country within the Community already had one! It was argued that if one wasn't started here there would be an increasing number of British citizens tempted by the prizes available in other countries. This would be made easier by the advance of technology and 'home shopping', making it more convenient for people to gamble from their own home, maybe even in secret.

In fact, all European countries are keen to ensure that their citizens do not participate in foreign lotteries because of the potential for corruption. Fairly recently, for example, it was reported that foreigners were being offered National Lottery tickets at a hugely inflated price. Advertisements in the United States and the Far East were offering people the chance to buy nine weekly £1 tickets for $65 – about £40. Camelot has been trying to locate who is behind these adverts which have appeared in a variety of publications. One advert in an airline's magazine gave an agent's address in Amsterdam. Camelot say that if such a scheme were being offered in Britain it would be illegal because the law states that a Lottery ticket cannot be traded at a profit. However, because the operations are based abroad, British legislation does not hold sway. Whether the schemes are illegal or not depends entirely on the country from which they are being organised. Whatever the case someone is obviously making a huge return.

This is not new. After the French Revolution the State Lottery was abolished. 'It is all the more dangerous since it devours the substance of the people and especially the poor', a leading opponent said. 'It was born of despotism and used to drown out the cry of misery, deluding the poor with false hope. The Lottery, an odious financial trick invades the

product of the poor man's toil and brings despair upon innumerable families.'

The reasons put forward for the Lottery

The main reason propounded for the introduction of the National Lottery was the need to provide extra funding for a whole range of valuable public enterprises which would otherwise entail an increase in the level of taxation. Certainly there has been some historical precedent in using large-scale lotteries for such a purpose – both the Sydney Opera House and the British Museum were established using this means of raising capital.

Most of us can sympathise with this sort of fund-raising, but it does raise two issues. First, it does need to be established that the Lottery will actually provide the extra funding. Any money that is spent buying lottery tickets will be money not spent on other items of expenditure. Therefore will the Lottery reduce charitable giving and/or will it reduce consumer spending? On the other hand it could simply increase personal debt as people buy lottery tickets with cash and then use credit for things such as food.

Secondly, although there is a public conception that the money raised goes to prizes and good causes there is also an inherent tax element. The Lottery is a form of regressive taxation even before the 12% is deducted (see below). It therefore needs to be seen for what it is – a source of revenue. That is why it is so important to analyse which groupings of people actually buy tickets because low-income earners can be particularly hard hit.

The amount raised

Before the Lottery began estimates of the turnover varied widely. The Government White Paper calculated its figure by comparing experiences in other European countries. It estimated that it might well take up to five years to reach maximum turnover which it then estimated would be at £3 - 4 billion pounds a year. However, when the Bill was actually announced the Heritage Secretary offered a lower figure of £2 - 3 billion. Other surveys carried out for the National Council of Voluntary Organisations (NCVO) and the Arts Council which were calculated by asking individuals in Britain indicated significantly lower figures. They estimated that there would be anything between £400 million and £1 billion available for good causes each year.

The White Paper also indicated that once the Lottery was well established one third, or 33%, of the revenue would be available for good causes. However, to help Camelot with start-up costs the actual initial breakdown of sales was decided as follows:

50%   Prizes
28%   Good causes (divided equally between the five different operating bodies)
12%   Tax
5%   Camelot Operating Costs
5%   Retailer Commission

Shifts in expenditure

It was felt important that before the Lottery was actually introduced a reasonably accurate picture was painted of where such resources would be diverted from. If, for example, the money were to be diverted from other forms of gambling such as the pools and bingo, there could be the collapse of much private enterprise in these areas with consequential large number of redundancies. Again if the money came as a result of a decrease in giving to good causes any positive impact that the National Lottery might have had would have been more than wiped out.

Extensive surveys were carried out by Saatchi and Saatchi which seemed to indicate that only a relatively modest amount of money spent on the Lottery would otherwise have been spent on other forms of gambling. The Gulbenkian Foundation, however, was not so sure. They argued that since the National Lottery closely mirrored the football pools in many of its essential characteristics there would be quite a high level of substitution. Their estimated proportions were as follows:

Reduced consumer spending elsewhere	35%
Existing savings	30%
Football pools	25%
Other gambling	10%

It is interesting to note that nowhere in either scenario is it suggested that indirectly people may borrow more to play the National Lottery.

Consequences for the football pools

Even taking a relatively low figure for annual turnover it was quickly realised that there could be significant pressure on the pools companies. If the National Lottery were going to be highly popular the potential damage could be calculated as catastrophic. Evidence from elsewhere in Europe indicates that this may well have been the case. Although the pools and the lottery have managed to co-exist in Italy, in all other countries the pools have been consistently squeezed out. A report by GAH Consultants suggested there would be a minimum of 1,100 job losses unless the Government offered some concessions (i.e. reduced betting duty).

These expected problems did cause some concern because it was not just a case of replacing one type of gambling with another. For a start there is a world of difference between a National Lottery which has the full promotion of the State behind it and the private promotion of the pools companies. On top of that the National Lottery would not employ very many people whereas pools companies are labour intensive and many are situated in areas of above-average unemployment. Also, if the pools companies' revenue did decline substantially it would have an adverse impact on their contribution to British football.

The effect on charitable giving

At the time of the Lotteries Bill the main concern of most charities was that their own direct income could drop as a result of a National Lottery, without a comparable return from the National Lotteries Board. They feared that this could be the case for a number of reasons.

First, people might substitute buying Lottery tickets for direct giving of existing donations; secondly, people would stop buying charitable lottery tickets when the National Lottery prizes were so much higher. The National Council of Voluntary Organisations (NCVO) calculated that there could well be a loss to the charitable sector of over £200 million and that approximately 7.5% of lottery income would be at the expense of charitable giving.

Obviously, these survey results are highly unreliable because people are often reluctant to admit that they would switch expenditure away from their charitable giving. However, historic precedent shows that this is very likely. Back in the 1930s there was clear evidence that the Irish

Hospitals Sweepstake had in fact caused many hospitals hardship because it resulted in a decline in direct charitable giving which could have been used for running costs whilst the sweepstake money was only available for specific 'concrete' projects. The NCVO has also cited recent evidence from Ireland, which has had a National Lottery since 1987, suggesting that about 10% of the money spent on the Lottery was at the expense of charitable giving whilst the sale of charitable lottery tickets fell by as much as 60%. It was thus calculated that a similar result here could mean an annual decline in charitable giving of £330 million. It is therefore probably this sort of figure that needs to be looked at and compared with the amount actually being given to charities (NOT all the good causes) before one can gauge how much, if at all, charities are actually benefiting.

Charities were also worried that the Lottery would lead to major redistribution of funding within the charitable sector and that this might well not reflect the merit or value of the work that such charities provided. Decisions would no longer be made individually but by a committee striving for fairness and balance. Even if this was achievable it was feared that some charities could undoubtedly lose out in a big way whilst others could be better resourced to win grants from the National Lotteries Charities Board.

Another cause for concern was that people would perceive that they were giving significantly to charity whenever they purchased a lottery ticket whereas only 28% goes to good causes and only 5.6% to the charities themselves. Thus, in encouraging people to participate in a lottery and thus significantly benefit charities, the Government, and for that matter, the operator could be accused of encouraging people to give inefficiently by misleading them about the actual net benefit to charities as well as encouraging a form of giving which prevents an on-going relationship developing between donor and charity.

The potential decline of Government funding

A number of charities expressed concern that the Government might use some of the money given for good causes for things which it would otherwise have had to fund itself. The Government acted quickly over this and pledged that no money available through the Lottery would be used to replace existing funding. It will, I believe, be interesting to see if this can be adhered to in difficult economic times when decisions have to be made in allocating rare resources. There has already been evidence of one minister, subsequently slapped down, suggesting that some of the monies raised could be used exactly for these purposes.

Experience in Ireland indicates that in times of severe economic difficulty about half the income given compensated beneficiaries for reduced exchequer spending during that period. There are also clear indications that many organisations which rely heavily on lottery funding in the United States are in financial difficulties. Part of the problem can be directly attributed to a decline in Government funding, although the erratic nature of the giving by the Lotteries Boards have also contributed to cash flow problems.

The pressures caused by 'indirect' taxation

As has been stated earlier, one of the major fears was that if all sectors of society bought the same number of lottery tickets this would, in percentage terms of real disposable income, significantly disadvantage the poorer members. This would be exacerbated if the Lottery then tended to fund projects which were of most benefit to those on higher incomes. Again to try and ascertain who would be interested in buying tickets Saatchi and Saatchi's survey indicated:

Socio-economic groupings			
AB	C1	C2	DE
36%	40%	45%	37%

These figures changed somewhat when it was pointed out
that some of the proceeds would go to good causes.

AB	C1	C2	DE
55%	53%	56%	42%

It is clear from the above that whilst there is some philanthropic interest from the ABs it matters little to the DEs. The
chance of winning increasingly becomes the sole motive for
participation as one moves down the social groupings.

Would those whose sole motive was winning be more
likely to be regular buyers of tickets, even though they had
the lowest disposable income? Evidence from abroad was not
encouraging. In the United States, of those who ever purchased lottery tickets, the top 10% in terms of frequency
bought 50% of the total number of tickets issued. Furthermore in some lotteries there were clear indications that there
was a high concentration of regular heavy betters in low
income groups. In Ireland the unemployed spend more on
the National Lottery than any other grouping.

This should be taken into account, I believe, when decisions are made as to where the Lottery money should go. It
can be rightly argued that sport, the arts and heritage do not
just benefit those who use them as a form of recreation and
entertainment. They can create jobs and boost tourism, for
example, which is for the general good of all parts of our
society. However, if the Sports and Arts Councils are committed to fund projects which should coincide with the contributions made by the various demographic groups they
need to tread carefully. It has been calculated that the AB
grouping participates in sport at a rate one-third above average and patronises the arts at over twice the average. Class E,
on the other hand, takes part in sport at one-third below
average and has only half the average involvement with the
arts. The Lotteries Bill does not take this into account at all.
It is probably why there has been such an outcry over some
of the awards made already, particularly by the Arts Council.

CHAPTER 2

WHAT ACTUALLY HAPPENED?

When the Lottery was launched in November 1994 it became abundantly clear that it would have a major impact on our society. As early as March 1995 Ray Stone wrote in *The Independent*, 'No single new product has ever had such a dramatic success in such a short time. Yet have we even begun to understand the implications of this, the biggest economic event since decimalisation? We have only just begun to trace the economic and social effects of this £3 billion business. Clearly Lottery mania is here to stay and is likely to grow steadily over the next few years, making ours the largest lottery in the world. It has flourished not despite, but because of the gloom still lingering from the recession of the early nineties.'

How well has it done?

By its first anniversary research showed that the National Lottery is now not only the biggest in the world but also makes the second highest contribution in tax and donations to good causes as a percentage of sales handing over 41% – just behind the New Jersey figure of 42%. Camelot has looked at most of the other lotteries in the world and come to the following conclusions:

Sales per employee   1st at £9.1 million

Contribution to Government
      on a per capita basis   12th
Operating expenses as a
      percentage of total revenue   13.1%

(This does not compare favourably with the lowest 6.8% of Puerto Rico or New Jersey at 8.3%.)

At the end of its first year Camelot had sold 4.5 billion £1 tickets for the on-line draw and 'scratch' cards. Prizes paid out were in the region of £2.1 billion, the five 'good causes' had benefited to the tune of more than £1.2 billion and the Treasury had collected £500 million in duty. In addition 132 millionaires were created in that first year.

On-line sales have continued to increase and moved up to £65.8 million on average over the last three months of its first operational year. To reach Camelot's five-year target however this figure will have to increase still further to around £100 million a week. Nevertheless the amount *currently* spent on the Lottery is equivalent of 0.5% of the nation's disposable income or 5% of our combined personal savings.

Camelot have admitted that the National Lottery has increased competition for other parts of the gambling industry but points out that thousands of jobs have been created and many small businesses have been rejuvenated. This is certainly true with some of the 20,000 shops and garages with Lottery terminals seeing sales rise by as much as 25%. Some food stores have also seen doubling of sales at their cigarette counters – and to this can be added the 5% pure profit that retailers keep from their ticket sales. Despite this, competitors not operating the Lottery do not seem to have been too adversely affected. This could be of course because non-Lottery purchasers will go elsewhere to avoid the queues!

It has been calculated that the Lottery is directly responsible for 10 million new shopping trips a week and 95% of people buying tickets claim they have not cut back elsewhere – so where is this £65 million a week coming from?

Who is playing?

Research indicates that about 65% of the adult British population play every week and that 90% have played at least once. Indications show that the socio-economic group DE play more regularly than any other. All groups seem to be spending roughly the same amount but that obviously gives a disproportionate picture in relation to the different incomes of these groups. Camelot divide the players as follows:

'Fun-loving moderates' – they enjoy spending	40%
Young under 35s who are 'the big prize dreamers' and thus playing for the jackpot	26%
'Anti-gamblers' who play because everyone else is and it is something to talk about	19%
The over 55s who play because it's something to do	15%

So far the lowest rate of winners compared to sums spent has been seen in Wales (33%) and the highest in Yorkshire (58%).

The odds of winning

Sadly, the chances of the 'big prize dreamer' actually seeing his fantasies fulfilled are remote. The odds on winning are roughly as follows:

(6 numbers) – Winning a jackpot in excess of £2 million (This compares with winning the pools jackpot at 1.2 million to 1.)	14 million to 1
(5 numbers) – Winning second prize (average £1500)	55,000 to 1
(4 numbers) – Winning third prize (average £65)	1,000 to 1

(3 numbers) – Winning fourth prize
   *(average £10)   57 to 1

The chances of winning the jackpot are far less likely than the chances of being struck by lightning. Given these odds perhaps it is not surprising that Neil Collins, City Editor of the *Daily Telegraph* wrote in November 1994, 'The real lottery winners will be those who do not enter and who are already far richer than most of those who do enter and lose, for the National Lottery is the most elegant way yet devised for taking money from the poor and redistributing it to the rich' (*Daily Telegraph*, 15 November 1994). Ladbrokes have licensed the chance of winning the Lottery jackpot as equivalent to Elvis landing a UFO on top of the Loch Ness Monster! More seriously, Ian Stewart, Professor of Maths at

In exceptional circumstances this prize may be scrapped.

the University of Warwick said, 'My problem is that the Lottery is what is known in the trade as a 'sucker-bet'. If a casino offered comparable odds it would be closed down.'

The Central Statistical Office (CSO) also assessed that the families that were playing the Lottery regularly were spending more on it than bread, newspapers or toiletries. In fact, the advent of the Lottery has caused the CSO to show spending on gambling separately for the first time.

The impact of gambling

A Mintel survey published in November 1995 found that pensioners and the low paid were in fact the most loyal participants in the National Lottery. 47% of those surveyed who bought tickets every week were from the C2 and D socio-economic groups. Furthermore 21% of those on a tight budget said they were still buying up to five tickets weekly.

The report also indicated that the National Lottery had encouraged 17% of those interviewed to participate in further forms of gambling. This coincided with comments from Gamblers Anonymous that they had seen a similar percentage increase in calls since the Lottery began. David Rigg, Camelot's Director of Communications, responded responsibly to this, 'I think there is quite a strong case for research into this area and we have been talking to some interested parties over a matter of months. We would be prepared to fund some of this research which must be done by an independent organisation which has the confidence of experts in this area, such as Gamblers Anonymous, so that it is credible.'

How Camelot have done

Camelot released their first set of trading figures on 21 November 1995. These showed interim profits for the twenty-four weeks to 16 September of £36.2 million on sales of £2.5 billion. These profits were defended by Tim Holley, their Chief Executive, as being 'less than one typical sales day on a Saturday'. They also need to be put into the context of necessary capital expenditure of £115 million and running costs of £82.7 million. Certainly they have established themselves very quickly and efficiently and it can be seen why they have received approaches from abroad to help set up lotteries in several overseas countries.

The impact on charities, sports and the arts

There was considerable criticism at the length of time the National Lottery Charities Board took to start making grants. This was primarily caused by cash flow problems at the charities themselves and was probably unfair. After all the Sports and Arts Councils and the Heritage Fund already existed and it would take time for the members of the Charities Board to meet and establish their giving priorities. Criteria also had to be drawn up by the Board's assessors before awards could be considered. These guidelines of assessment fell into four categories – policy, potential achievements, management and long-term viability.

First, applicants would be asked whether their initiatives fitted in with the Board's policy priorities. So, for example, the initial handouts in late 1995 concentrated on poverty whilst those in Spring 1996 will focus on health and disability, as well as British charities working abroad. At this stage Board assessors will evaluate the degree to which the charity's proposed activity involves users and beneficiaries in its development and management, encourages community participation and fosters self-help or improvement. They will also consider how well planned the proposal is, so applicants need to demonstrate that their scheme is well-managed and financially sound, well planned, staffed appropriately, cost-effective, good value for money, committed to equal opportunities and able to involve volunteers effectively.

Finally, other factors which may affect the long-term success of the scheme will be looked at. They may, for example, consider the presence of strategic and innovative thinking – i.e. does the activity reflect new ways of thinking about existing problems, will there be sustainable benefit to people or communities who participate, has the activity the potential to be seen as a pilot or model of good practice, and will the activity be able to continue once the funding ends?

Successful applicants will then be monitored in two ways. First, the Board will require progress reports from organisations. Secondly, it will be able to make random, spot checks or request additional information to ensure that all the money is being spent appropriately.

Members of the National Lottery Charities Board

The Charities Board has twenty-one members representing England, Wales, Scotland and Northern Ireland who are picked by ministers from industry, academia and charities. The Board is led by David Sieff, a director of Marks and Spencer plc and a member of the Council for Industry of the Prince's Youth Business Trust. At the time of writing the other twenty members were as follows:

Tessa Baring	Chairman of the Association of Charitable Foundations, part-time Charity Commissioner, Trustee of Barnados
Amir Bhatia	Charity worker with ethnic minorities, unemployed and hospices. An Oxfam Trustee
Graham Bowie	Former Chief Executive of Lothian Regional Council – involved in voluntary work with HIV/AIDS sufferers
Ian Clarke	Ex-Bank of England, Council Member of the University of Newcastle, Non-Executive Director of a hospital trust
Stella Clarke	JP, Deputy Lieutenant of Avon, Chairman of Council of Bristol University

June Churchman	Vice-President of the Guides Association and Wales Voluntary Youth Services
Alan Higgins	Retired teacher and HM Inspector of Schools, Chair of Welsh Association of Youth Clubs
Tom Jones	Farmer, Member of the Country-side Council for Wales and on Agricultural Training Board
Amanda Jordan	Senior Executive National Westminster Bank and Chair of their Charitable Trust
Julia Kaufmann	Director BBC Children in Need, works with Association of Charitable Foundations and Gingerbread
William Kirkpatrick	Member of Gaming Board and former JP
Philomena De Lima	Psychology lecturer and works with community development projects
Aideen McGinley	Involved in rural and community development work
Monica McWilliams	Lecturer in Social and Community Science, works with youth and women's organisations
Andrew Phillips	Solicitor specialising in charity law
Linda Quinn	Expert on drugs abuse, works in prisons
Sir Adam Ridley	Board Member of Hambros Bank and Member of Council of Charitable Support
John Simpson	Political adviser on job creation, economics lecturer, probation work

Noel Stewart	Chartered accountant, hospital trust chairman, Hon Treasurer Queens University, Belfast
Chris Woodcock	Head of Corporate Affairs Kelloggs, member of a community development trust

CHAPTER 3

THE GREAT DEBATE

A t this stage, before looking at individual winners and
losers, it is worth considering various standpoints.
With 54% of the general public saying in a recent survey that they now talked more about the Lottery than the
state of the British weather there is obviously much to dis-
cuss! David McKie in a thought-provoking article in the
Guardian in November 1995 described the National Lottery
as a 'theatre of the burlesque, a conduit of mass escapism – a
new religion even'. He went on, 'It's become an essential part
of the nation's Saturday night. Theatres and cinemas suffered
as the world began to tune in to Anthea Turner. Even emi-
nent figures are hooked. "I buy a weekly ticket in a
newsagent in my constituency" Sir Ivan Lawrence
(Conservative: Burton) told a Commons debate on the
Lottery on 25 October. "There is always a queue for tickets.
The people in that queue are always delighted to see
me...people get fun out of the Lottery not just from watching the programme in the evening but from putting their
money on and winning a tenner here or there". Sir Ivan puts
on a fiver a week. He has won eight times netting some £80.
It has cost him £140-£150. Happy Sir Ivan! Like so many
others he's a loser who feels a winner.

'But in Mrs Bottomley's Lottery everybody starts as equal
competitors – unlike the wider lottery that is life – are not
boosted or handicapped by the accident of birth, by strong
or feeble physique, by good looks or the lack of them. This

makes success more acceptable. Many…show no resentment at all against those who grow rich through the Lottery. Family and friends [especially the long-lost friends who turn up on winners' doorsteps to offer congratulations and ask for a share themselves] may persecute the successful but people in pubs and clubs are generally philosophical. Good luck to them, they will say. It could have been me. Perhaps one day it will be…The Lottery has given the whole nation a whole new soap opera. There are some you celebrate with and some you love to hate.'

Let's have a look now at some of the different positions.

The Government

Not surprisingly the Government, having promoted the Lottery, is supporting it fully, in public at least. Virginia Bottomley, the Minister for National Heritage, said the average weekly spend of just over £2 was 'less than a packet of cigarettes' and she denied it was exploiting the people least able to afford it. Calling it 'harmless fun' she described it as the most successful lottery of all time, having generated more money more quickly than any other lottery in history. Mrs Bottomley, who says she plays the Lottery as part of a family syndicate, also denied that it had created gambling mania in Britain. She believes that warnings do not need to be given as there are many ways people can spend money unwisely. 'I don't think we can be that much of a nanny,' she said. Money remained the uppermost thought in her mind apparently when she also defended the size of the jackpots. 'If you want to have a maximum return to good causes, all the evidence is that the big jackpots are what make more people play. 10-20% more comes in for the good causes when you have a big jackpot,' she said at the same time dismissing calls for raising the age limit of sixteen for buying tickets. Nevertheless Mrs Bottomley did rule out a 'double roll-over' jackpot that was proposed by Camelot for their first anniversary on the grounds that it was too controversial given the criticisms and also that the planned event was timed to coincide with Remembrance Day.

And behind the scenes too there has been the odd sign of Tory dissatisfaction in the way in which the Lottery has been run. Hugh Colver resigned in November 1995 as Director of Communications of the Tory Party saying that 'the National Lottery is an example of how to turn a public relations triumph into a disaster.'

There are, of course, other and not very altruistic reasons why the Government welcomes the Lottery. Over several years the Exchequer may pick up more than £1 billion in revenue duties. This tax goes largely unmentioned in all the Lottery discussions. It is hidden behind a steady stream of good news of charitable giving. Every round of successful applicants for Lottery funding – as long as they are for perceived deserving causes rather than things like the Churchill Papers or Sadler's Wells – is evidence of good and relief from more gloomy stories elsewhere in the press. Furthermore, without the Lottery there would have been little money to celebrate the Millennium – whereas now the construction of the first monuments have already started.

There have already too been fears that some Lottery cash would replace public sector spending. William Waldegrave, the Chief Secretary to the Treasury, was quick to deny that letters exchanged between Virginia Bottomley and himself meant that he was advocating substituting Lottery cash for Government spending. This would have broken the Prime Minister's pledge that all Lottery funds would be in addition to existing public spending plans. However, because of international convention, Lottery financing is classed as part of general Government spending so there are inherent dangers of some gentle drift. One example of this came when the Welsh Tourist Office withdrew its offer of funding to the Brecon Jazz Festival because the other half of its funding was provided by the Lottery. The rules are that the State pump-primes such charities leaving the charity to find the other half of the cash required from the private sector. But because Lottery funding is regarded as Government funding the

Lottery can provide half or the Welsh Tourist Board can provide half but they can't both provide half as they are both
public-spending agencies!

In a nutshell the Tory Government has pledged to keep
things as they are.

The Labour Party

The Labour Party has been critical of some aspects of the
way the Lottery is run. Hardly surprisingly they are critical
of the level of profitability of Camelot and indicated that
they would be looking for a non-profit making operator.
Jack Cunningham, the Shadow National Heritage Secretary,
called for a shake-up saying, 'These profits are excessive by
any standards. Camelot has a licence to print tickets and
another to print money. It is another private monopoly set
up by a Conservative Government which is making excessive
profits.' He also said he would be setting up an independent
inquiry to advise on the issues thrown up by the success of
the Lottery. These will include the questions of underage
gambling and how to distribute funds fairly to compensate
charities whose fund-raising has suffered.

They have also been critical of the moves to introduce the
Lottery into pubs – a move that originated from both the
beer industry and confectionery and tobacco suppliers who
have lost out to consumers buying scratch cards with their
loose change rather than chocolates or cigarettes. Dr
Cunningham thought this move raised serious questions
about the running of the game. 'Alcohol and gambling often
do not mix well...under-age gambling and under-age drinking may well be facilitated by the installation of Lottery
machines in pubs', he said, feeling that this matter should be
looked at by Oflot before it was allowed to happen. In the
Parliamentary debate in October 1995 the National Lottery
was described as a 'poll tax in carpet slippers' and Mr Robert
McCartney argued that 'the greatest amount of money is
being spent on the Lottery in such poor areas because it

offers a dream or a hope which the Government does not offer through employment and thrift.'

The Liberal Democrat Party

Robert Maclennan, Liberal Democrat Heritage spokesman, also said it was 'shameless' that Camelot had announced such profits when many charities were still suffering funding shortfalls because of the operation of the Lottery. They also tabled a motion, backed by Labour, saying that Camelot should be required to open its books to the National Audit Office, the public finance watchdog. They are concerned that shareholders in Camelot have enjoyed double profits – through contracts to supply computer terminals and printed entry slips as well as sharing dividends for example.

Camelot

Camelot has been delighted by the Lottery's performance so far and has no plans to amend what it sees as a successful operation. Furthermore, even though sales have been above expectations they have been planning another televised Lottery draw mid-week should there be any signs of sales flagging. Tim Holley, Chief Executive, said 'The mid-week draw is one of the options we have but there are lots of other games we are looking at too. We want to keep sales at the same level or with a slow level of growth.'

David Rigg, Director of Communications, stoutly defends their position, 'We put in the lowest bid. We charged less than the other competitors.' Profits are not excessive either, he argues. 'It is an extraordinarily low figure even for a high volume, low-risk business.' Even supermarkets which are low-risk thanks to their selling the bare necessities of life, like food, do not have such a small margin,' he said. But supermarkets of course have on-going capital costs which Camelot do not. Bank credit facilities of up to £75 million have barely been touched since launch.

Mr Rigg also says that, like supermarkets, Camelot is

operating in a competitive environment. When it was put to him that Camelot were the only company with a licence and thus a monopoly provider that could not fail, especially with the enormous media coverage, Mr Rigg defended Camelot's record. 'Back in May 1994 when we won the licence and six months before launch we said sales would peak at £5.5 billion a year with a total of £9 billion (over the period of the licence) going to good causes. The great majority of commentators said it was unachievable.' He also pointed out that there would have been heavy penalties if the launch had had to be delayed. 'I am not sympathetic to the view any fool could do it and it is money for old rope. Since we spend most time in this country moaning about great British cock-ups it is refreshing to have something that has gone spectacularly right,' he said. It has certainly gone right for Mr Rigg too. He receives a salary of approximately £150,000 with 50% more due to the bonus payable to all Camelot executives for achieving launch on the due date, another 50% for exceeding annual targets and a further 140% under a long-term incentive scheme.

The Church

There have always been difficulties in getting the Church to speak with one voice and their reaction is looked at more closely in a later chapter. Nevertheless, at the time of the Lottery's first anniversary most denominations were united in condemning it. Their spokesman, the Rt Revd David Sheppard, Anglican Bishop of Liverpool, called for an investigation into the Lottery. 'Gambling is being encouraged and artificially stimulated,' he said. 'The scratch cards are driving a coach and horse through all the rules of gambling.' Attacking this huge new invasion in our life, he was especially critical of the 'extreme hype of Saturday nights.' He was particularly concerned about the BBC's Lottery show being the second most popular programme among children and said the age limit for buying tickets should be raised from sixteen to eighteen because children as young as eleven had been found playing. Calls for the jackpot to be capped and a reduced number of outlets were also supported.

Arts/Charities

The first distribution of grants by the five different bodies gave plenty of ammunition to critics who had predicted that the Lottery would emerge as a 'tax on the poor to fund the pastimes of the rich'. Among the most prominent grants are £55 million to redevelop the Royal Opera House in London, £50 million for a new modern art museum, £30 million for the Sadler's Wells Foundation, £15.8 million for the Royal Court Theatre and £13.3 million to buy the Churchill Papers which many people thought already belonged to the nation. However despite all the publicity, of which most was adverse, only 30% of the grants made so far have been for more than £1 million. More than two-thirds are both below £100,000 and outside the capital. There has, however, been concern that many needy causes, especially in the inner cities, have not benefited.

There is also a fear, already mentioned and discussed further in Chapter 5, that many charities have, and will, suffer a decline in giving and therefore little by little their range of activity may have to be reduced. Giving would already appear to be down around 15% and falling. Unless this message can be clearly got across there will be many who feel they are doing enough for charities by simply buying Lottery tickets. Camelot have subsequently advertised that the best way to help charities is by giving direct.

The National Lottery Charities Board

David Sieff is the first Chairman of the National Lottery Charities board. His ambition is 'to create a humane and approachable organisation that is judged by the quality of its grants and how they touch people.' His role has been to get fellow board members to recognise that they are there to serve the national interest as opposed to just their own specialised areas of knowledge. He is reasonably happy with the progress so far. He said, 'Don't forget that when I started we had absolutely nothing, no structure, no board members, nothing. Today we have a staff of 102 and we are putting in place nine regional managers to improve communications.'

Mr Sieff is very clear that the charities he would like to see benefit most from the grants are those that are least able to raise funds. What works best with applications, he says is not brilliant presentation but the quality of the activity. 'What we are hoping to move towards is a balance of grants dependent on type, size and geographical area.' He is also concerned about a proliferation of charities trying to do virtually the same thing. In these cases he suggests that it could well be in their interests to get together and apply as one.

Regarding the various controversies and criticisms Mr Sieff is probably most dismissive of the complaint about the focus being on poverty. 'We did an enormous amount of consulting about this. But remember the focus will grow as we grow. This is why youth was added to poverty in the second round of grants for example.' He is, however, not so dismissive of charities suffering through the Lottery and expressed his sympathy whilst also pointing out that there are, in fact, some charities whose funds have actually risen. Mr Sieff is also very emphatic the Government should not allow funds from the Lottery to replace existing funding. 'It's illegal,' he said. 'I will be keeping a watchful eye on it.'

The press

Since the National Lottery started it has been hard to find a newspaper which does not have some story about it. Some have been praiseworthy, many critical and quite a few have overly focused on the personal details of the winners. Will Hutton in a piece in the *Guardian* confirmed surveys that nearly 90% of people interviewed approved of the Lottery. He wrote, 'The National Lottery is a means of redistributing from the poor to the rich while giving the Treasury a hand-some bonus on the way. Yet to criticise the Lottery is to court the accusation of being a killjoy. The audiences for the Saturday evening National Lottery Live may be falling and the demand for 'instants' [the Lottery scratch cards] begin-ning to subside but the Lottery has won its place in the nation's affection. If our fellow countrymen and women wish to play a game of hazard where the chances of winning the jackpot are only marginally higher than being hit by a mete-orite, then it's a "harmless flutter". And the money does go to good causes, doesn't it? Despite the manufactured outrage over Covent Garden or Sadler's Wells receiving millions, more than a billion has been found for other causes. There is a general sense, broadly correct, that most of them are thor-oughly deserving.'

In a brilliant article in the *Daily Telegraph* Boris Johnson looked at our own hypocrisy and double-standards, our prej-udices, our ability to criticise things we know little about and yet ignore things that we know are factually correct. The arti-cle was written on the day the National Lottery Charities Board made its first payout and it is so good, and funny, I find it hard to leave much out!

You couldn't make it up, the tabloid commentators rave to themselves in an ecstasy of indignation. Gorblimey. You Could Not Make It Up. And you might agree with them that the National Lottery is turning into a mad new Common Agricultural Policy of misdirected cheques. With one hand it appears to shower subsidy on fat Italians in tights, sponsoring young men of dubious tastes to prance around in tutus, as well as the pseuds in cummer-bunds who watch them. And with the other hand as the *Sunday Express* elegantly put it yesterday, it doles out money to immigrants, single mothers, heroin addicts, winos and all manner of Political Correctness. You might be in full agreement with the professional splutterers that it is outrageous that a 'toffs' redoubt like the Royal Opera House should receive £78 million from the Lottery. You might find it preposterous that £12.5 million should have been spent to keep the Churchill Papers in the country when we, the public, thought we owned them anyway. You might be gagging in fury that a bunch of Tory quangocrats is currently deciding how to spend about £1.5 billion of Lottery revenue taken from the pockets of ordinary punters who have foregone crisps and cigarettes to take part in the game.

Before you burst a blood vessel though let us contemplate the mind-blowing hypocrisy of this debate...If you tell me that when we all queue up at the newsagent or petrol station and, trembling, scratch out the six numbers according to our wives' birthdays at that moment uppermost in our thought is the heart-warming prospect that 28p in the pound will go on 'good causes'. If you tell me that I will say, sorry old son I simply do not believe you.

In that instant we do not care one whit whether 0.05p of our stake goes to the Eritrean Advice and Information Centre or for Save the Children. What concerns us is whether we are about to become millionaires while doing nothing to deserve it and luxuriating in fantasy about how we would spend the money. For this is gambling. And were we gambling in anything else we would not morally expect to have any say in how the bookies invested our accumulated losses...The Tory Government has nationalised a large chunk of the gaming sector and deemed that 12p in every pound shall go to the Treasury. The Lottery is therefore more like a tax. It is not a tax on earnings, or on sales since nothing worthwhile is bought. It is a tax on stupidity. It is an impost on the credulity and optimism of those who believe they will prevail over odds of 13,983,813 to one and win the 'jackpot'.

The remit of the National Lottery Charities Board is to "help meet the needs of those at greatest disadvantage in society"...It is a mistake to attack these curious little groups merely for their names. We saw what an ass Dr Brian Mawhinney accidentally made of himself when he attacked the Camden Hopscotch Asian Women's Group which turned out to be run by Save the Children which has the Princess Royal as its patron. And if you say there are other national charities more deserving that look to the health, old age and infirmity of all our people you are of course right. And all these charities shall receive their money...

...There remains one course open to those who froth at funding Eritreans. The Lottery is unlike a normal tax in the crucial respect that we do not have to pay it. There is a simple way of ensuring that your money goes to a national medical charity and that is to avoid the Lottery and give the money direct. That way the charity receives a full pound of your money not a fraction of a penny and you will cease to be tormented by the delusion that you are about to become a millionaire!

[Boris Johnson, *Daily Telegraph*, October 1995]

Joe Rogaly wrote in the *Financial Times* in June 1995, 'The British National Lottery is an outrage, a swindle, a confidence trick, a Treasury romp, a waste of money, a senseless diversion for a tired nation. Worst of all it is enormously popular.'

Others

Joan Bakewell (TV presenter)
'The judgemental tone of the tabloids has deluded the public into regarding this as some sort of tax over which they have rights to decide how it is distributed. I rejoice with the Royal Opera House and Sadler's Wells as much as with Hayling Island Amateur Dramatic Society.'

Richard Branson
Mr Branson, whose own bid to run the Lottery on a non-profit basis was pipped by Camelot and who has thus been described by Mrs Bottomley as a 'disappointed loser', has said it is time to change the rules. He believes that, as Camelot will make far more money than it predicted from a

monopoly licence to print money, the time has come for everyone to consider seriously how the charities that have suffered from the National Lottery could benefit from such huge windfall monopoly profits.

Jim McCormick
As reviewer of a survey by the Institute of Political Research of lotteries worldwide he concluded that the public in Britain should have a much greater involvement in where the money goes in relation to the good causes as they do elsewhere in Europe. It comes down, he thinks, to accountability in involving citizens much more.

Alan Bleasdale (playwright)
'My instinctive moral horror at the Lottery is relived every Saturday in newsagents throughout the land as the worn-out, the elderly, the shabby and the desperate queue up in the hope of their only escape. I also know that every small charity that myself and my friends are involved with has lost out.'

Max Clifford (public relations consultant)
'I don't do the Lottery. My father was a big gambler and as a result I have an insight into the world of winners and losers'.

Jenny Diski (novelist)
'I have a great respect for fantasy. But the best fantasies must have at least a remote chance of being fulfilled so at odds of 14 million to 1 I haven't bothered to buy a ticket.'

Mark Wallinger (artist)
'I hate the Lottery because it is a tax on the poor and gullible. I hate Camelot, the most charmless company ever created. Giving money to Eton and the Churchills is an obscenity. And most of all I hate it because I've lost fourteen quid on the bastard thing.'

Peregrine Worsthorne (newspaper columnist)
'I am totally in favour. It seems to give the masses a lot of instant pleasure without doing any harm. I suppose you

could say it has replaced religion as the new opiate of the people.'

The general public

Nearly all who buy tickets dream of winning. What they would do with the money is varied. Below is just a sample of comments from various people who have been interviewed.

- Foster parents said it was the only way they could raise £1 million to start a home for deprived children. They use a keyring to pick their numbers and spend £5 a week but so far they have won nothing.

- A thirty-year-old lady's first priority would be to 'have her boobs enlarged' – although she also wants a country house, antiques, designer clothes, jewellery, a Jaguar and two Lamborghinis. If the Lottery ended she would not know what to do. 'The live draw has become the highlight of my week,' she said.

- A barmaid would want to buy her council house and take her family round the world. She chooses her numbers by studying her tropical fish. She claims their droppings often make the shape of numbers which she writes down and uses.

What is perhaps worrying about all this dreaming is that doctors have now identified a new delusional illness triggered by publicity about the National Lottery. In June 1995 the *Times* reported that 'Lottomania' has affected two London women who needed hospital treatment and drugs after becoming convinced that they had won the Lottery jackpot. One of the women believed that she had won £2 million and became upset when staff at her building society said they had no record of her large deposit. Both women were convinced they were being threatened by neighbours who were trying to deprive them of their winnings. Dr Harry Doyle, a consultant psychiatrist at Harrow Hospital, said he thought such delusions would become increasingly common. 'I'm sure plenty of people are addicted. The fear is that if you stop that is the week that your number will come up.'

CHAPTER 4

THE EFFECTS ON THE 'WINNERS' AND 'LOSERS'

The Lottery has made millionaires of over 130 people since it started. As a total they are not yet making much impact in the amazing number of 49,000 millionaires in Britain but over time their percentage will surely grow. At least now big winners should be able to receive the anonymity which was singularly lacking for some of the earlier winners. For those early winners a combination of in-depth research and 'digging up the dirt' probably made many of them feel like losers.

As a result new measures were taken by Camelot and the press in April 1995 to protect the anonymity of winners who did not wish their identity to be revealed. At the same time the office of the National Lottery published its investigations into how the name of the first major jackpot winner of £17.8 million in December 1994 came to be revealed. Although Oflot found no evidence that Camelot breached its operating licence it put forward a series of 'lessons for the future'. These include:

- The provision of firm and unequivocal advice on how winners should conduct themselves in the crucial hours after a top prize has been won.

- Camelot should provide ways of validating winning tickets without requiring the holders to visit buildings likely to be watched by the press.

- Camelot should also offer options for transferring winnings to unidentified bank accounts.

The Press Complaints Commission also said that if National Lottery winners wanted to remain anonymous the press should generally respect that desire. The warning came as the Commission issued its own guidelines on the coverage of Lottery winners following complaints about the conduct of several newspapers which named the December 10th winner.
These new guidelines include:

- A ban on practices such as offering money for information about Lottery winners.

- The press should not try to obtain information on winners by harassing family and neighbours.

- Newspapers could identify winners who wanted privacy only if it was in the public interest.

The Commission added that the press could not be expected to 'act as a scapegoat in maintaining the anonymity of winners irrespective of all circumstances, including the actions of Camelot or the winners themselves.' They concluded with regard to the events of December 10th that because of the actions of Camelot 'some journalists were encouraged to search for and narrow down a list of possible people who were recipients of the large prize.'
Certainly the winner of this enormous jackpot did not suddenly find that his life had become a bed of roses. The Asian factory worker and his family hailed from Blackburn and were described by Camelot on receipt of their prize as 'a delightful family who had reacted very well to this incredible news.' Following the news of his win he was ostracised by his workmates and had to flee the country for two months after being condemned by fellow Muslims for gambling. He has moved to the Home Counties under an assumed name and separated (albeit temporarily) from his wife.
There have been other winners who have been pilloried in the press and who must question how much of that was fair.

It became common knowledge, to the extent that a film was made about him, that one young man from Leicestershire who won £6.5 million in March 1995 was facing court charges. Jobless at the time of his win, he bought a farm-house for £1 million and proved to be an unusually extrava-gant winner by also buying a Rolls Royce, a Bentley, a Ferrari, a Porsche and a helicopter. However, the young man concerned will be unable to use these for a while as in August 1995 he received an eighteen months' prison sentence for handling stolen vehicles before his jackpot win.

A thirty-three year old man from Hastings who worked as a double glazing salesman also got more than he bargained for when he won half of the largest jackpot so far, £22.5 million. His estranged, third wife immediately put in a claim for half his fortune but was eventually reportedly paid £1 million on their divorce. He was also called a 'lying two-faced bas-tard' by a string of former wives and girlfriends – even his mother had nothing good to say about him. Things got so bad that one national tabloid actually ran a feature asking if anyone knew anything good about him. The man in question has said that he has had beer poured over him by people call-ing him a 'rich bastard' and said he felt like a prisoner because of his fame. However it is reported that he managed to clinch a newspaper deal on his fourth wedding.

Another smaller winner of £50,000, a mother of five, has said that she now would happily have burnt her prize. She is quoted as saying 'I'm a loser in all this. It should have bought me so much happiness.' After winning she became embroiled with a man who was rapidly to become her former boyfriend when he claimed he was entitled to half her winnings. Eventually she paid £13,000 in an out-of-court settlement but during the dispute she claims mystery callers phoned up to thirty times, some making death threats against her chil-dren.

A young couple who won £265,000 also believes the money has done them more harm than good. They had to move to a secret address after being hounded by neighbours for a share of their big win. The couple, who have two young children, also had to endure crank calls and prowlers. The winner's mother said, 'People kept trying to break into the house and friends were dropping by asking for money.' In desperation the family had to quit their £40 a week council home and move to a hideaway several miles away.

One forty-two-year-old Yorkshireman who lists his most compelling passion as 'drinking beer' has apparently already got bored with his £1.4 million Lottery win. He says he wants to go back to work. 'There are times I wish I had never seen the money,' he said. 'Life is such a drag now that I can afford anything I want. Now we don't have to scrimp and save everything is too easy. Life has lots its buzz and to be honest it's all a bit boring.' So far he has spent a few hundred pounds on 'drinks for the lads', had two short breaks in Skegness and bought a second-hand television. They have also paid cash for a new bungalow worth £64,000 but he claims they only moved because he had cabbages stolen from his garden at their previous home. The only extravagance in sight is a Mercedes which will be bought when his drink-driving ban has expired. He is now looking for a job. As his wife said, 'Most people would be content to sit back and enjoy the win but not him. I think the money was doing his head in.'

It must be stated, however, that many people do enjoy their winnings. Most new Lottery millionaires remain cautious, invest about two-thirds of their winnings, limit big spending to new houses and cars and half have not given up their jobs. Of those who continue to work 17% have stayed in the same job while 33% have started new positions after clearing their existing debts. For example, among the new working millionaires is a sub-postmaster from Alloa in Scotland who retired with his wife to buy a local hotel. He said, 'The best thing about winning the Lottery is knowing your children will be secure and even more so your grandchildren because you wonder what kind of jobs are going to be out there for them in the future. They are going to reap the benefits of this.' So far their most expensive purchase has been a new BMW which they intended to buy anyway. They have no intention of moving house and have no plans for a holiday.

Other happy winners include an ex-trucker of sixty-three who celebrated his £6.6 million win by moving to a caravan in Wales! They moved there temporarily while their end-of-terrace house in Manchester was being re-wired and re-decorated. He splashed out on a new Jaguar, a home for his wife's mother and gave each of his sons £1 million. The rest has been invested. He said, 'We have all got nice cars now. But apart from that we've all very much still got our feet on the ground and we're all still happy.'

An antique dealer from Plymouth who won £2.4 million has also remained living above his shop with his mother and brother. His one obvious concession to luxury was to buy a second-hand Mercedes but he has invested substantial amounts in land and other businesses.

Another successful winner was already a millionaire businessman who won £1.2 million. He said the best thing about winning the Lottery is the feeling that the threat of losing everything has gone.

A new car is the most popular purchase with 68% of winners buying at least one. About half bought a new house for themselves with 10% buying one for someone else. Just over half almost immediately took a holiday. On average the big winners have given away 14% of their winnings. A survey of big winners showed that they regarded the three best things about winning the Lottery as:

• financial security

• helping family and friends

• the ability to fulfil lifetime ambitions

When winners are given their cheques they are advised to go on holiday immediately and spend nothing until the shock has sunk in. Incidentally, the most popular destinations are Barbados, the Bahamas and Disneyland.

But there are very big winners who spend very little. One young lady from East London won £14 million. She bought her parents a Ford Escort and continues to live with them. And a young man who won £5 million made only one immediate purchase – a season ticket for his football club – Doncaster Rovers.

Yet despite their caution winners of the jackpot say their biggest regrets are that they didn't win more and they didn't win sooner.

Other winners

The 132 millionaires	If your name is John, you're a builder and in your thirties you are a composite jackpot winner. The luckiest name so far has been John [would my brother and chairman please take note!] and most winners have been manual workers in the construction industry. Winners are, on average, thirty-four years old. Perhaps because of their jobs home improvements were a priority. Sadly, only one out of 120 told Camelot that any of the windfall was going to charity.
The shareholders of Camelot	
The Board of Camelot	Chief Executive Tim Holley received £330,000 in its first year of operation.
The Treasury	The Lottery has raised approximately £500 million.
Those living in the Midlands	
	Fifty-three jackpot winners (average £715,000) so far.
Good causes	Large sums have already been spent by all five bodies. Among the biggest winners are the Tate Gallery (£50m), the Earth Centre

	Doncaster (£50m), the National Cycle Network (£42.5m), Portsmouth Harbour (£40m) and Sadler's Wells (£30m).
London	Has 12% of the population but has also received one-third of the grants.
'High culture'	With so much going to the Royal Opera House and other similar projects it is clear that a high percentage of the giving benefits people who enjoy the arts.
The Churchill Family	£12.5 million paid for the Churchill archives – bought for the nation.
Las Vegas	Since the National Lottery started Thomas Cook has reported a 20% increase and British Airways a 44% increase in holidays to Las Vegas.
Mystic Meg	Ex-writer of soft pornography, now a national TV star with Saturday night forecasts.
National Lottery Enterprises	
	Makers of Lottery pens, books, calculators and computer programmes.
Small charities	such as the Crouch End Clock Tower Centenary Celebration Committee and the Bingham Infants Self-Help Group.
Modest community and arts projects	
	Among these – many saved from the brink – is Zippo's Academy of Circus Art. This is a travelling school providing training in circus skills which received £48,000 for a new tent. 'We had run out of people to ask for more money and there's no doubt the school would have been forced to close if we hadn't

had this grant. The Lottery has saved the circus school,' said the manager of the Academy.

Brass bands

A host of brass bands, once supported by the mining industry, have been helped by the Lottery. The Morecambe Youth Band received £48,000 for new instruments. 'When it costs £5,000 to buy a new tuba and you only get £200 for a park concert how do you survive?' said Bernard Vause, musical director of the band. 'We were thrilled. The Lottery is providing people like us with money that was never dreamed of.'

Other losers

Family going on holiday

A man was waiting with his family at Newcastle airport for a flight to the Canary Islands. He went into the newsagents and bought some scratch cards. When he found he hadn't won anything he bought more and more. Even when he won small amounts he used the cash to buy more cards. Eventually he completely cleared the shop of instant cards. Even allowing for the small sums he had won he had spent £490 on nothing.

Man who committed suicide

A fifty-one year old father of two very tragically killed himself directly as a result of the National Lottery. He bought tickets in advance, always using the same numbers. One Sunday in April 1992 he came to check his ticket and believed he had got all six numbers correct and that he stood to win over £1 million. It then dawned on him that he didn't have a valid ticket for that week. In shock he went upstairs and shot himself. In fact only four of his numbers had come up and so in reality he had deprived his family of a husband and father for £27. A police source said, 'The man had obviously flipped. He was a church-goer and a very fine man with no dark side to his character. You can never judge what people are capable of at times of stress.' A neighbour said, 'He was the nicest man in our street. He worked for the church and was always visiting the sick.' However, perhaps the most enlightening comments came from the man's newsagent from whom he bought the Lottery tickets. He said, 'The National Lottery does strange things to people. They become obsessed. For some of my customers it is all they seem to live for. They spend their last pennies on it each week. It is very said that these are the extremes gambling can lead to.'

Richard Branson
The running of the National Lottery was not awarded to him.

Northern Ireland
Only nine big winners at the time of writing.

Some winners!

It would appear that many people do not even check their tickets to see if they have won. There is over £22 million outstanding in unclaimed prizes. The biggest winning ticket so far unclaimed is £259,251.

Gamblers Anonymous

Since the National Lottery started calls to Gamblers Anonymous have increased by 17% and are rising. Personality tests indicate that there are up to 1.7 million people with the potential to become problem gamblers. The National Lottery appears to be flushing out quite a few of them. Traditional gambling facilities were designed to respond to unstimulated demand so there was little or no advertising. But National Lottery's high profile has turned people into gamblers who had never even had a flutter before. Gamblers Anonymous have voiced 'great concern' at the numbers of people who are getting hooked on the Lottery and the purchase of instant or 'scratch' cards. They claim to be seeing children as young as eleven buying and getting addicted to scratch cards. At Credit Action we have received Lottery-related calls on our debt helpline. One lady told how she had bought clothes for her children from a catalogue and had got into debt because her husband had been spending the repayment money on Lottery tickets. Other agencies undoubtedly will have similar stories to tell.

Some charities

There has been quite a shortfall in giving. Estimates have been made that over £200 million of charitable giving has been diverted into buying Lottery tickets. Even allowing for grants received from the National Lottery there is likely to be a significant shortfall – in the region of £90 million in the first year according to the NCVO.

Medical charities

These were excluded from the first round of grant-making and have also therefore suffered losses.

The less well-off

According to Camelot a person in social class DE spends as much on the Lottery each week (average £2.30) as a person in class AB. This figure represents a much higher percentage of the poorer person's income. However, a Mintel survey found the situation to be even worse than this. In a survey for *This Sunday* it found that those with an annual income of between £5,000 and £10,000 spend an average of £6.52 a week – a total of £338 a year. The report, compiled from interviews with 180 people in three inner-city areas of Manchester came after church leaders had expressed concern about the effect of the Lottery on the 'most vulnerable in society'. The survey also showed:

Income £20,000 – £30,000
   average spent on Lottery and instants: £3 a week
Income £15,000 – £20,000
   average spent on Lottery and instants: £3.80 a week
Income £10,000 – £15,000
   average spent on Lottery and instants: £4.16 a week

People on benefit also spent an average of £4.16 a week which equates to more than £200 a year. The National Lottery is thus increasingly being seen as the only way out for many poorer families.

A chauffeur

In August 1995 a twenty-six year old man became the first person to stand trial for swindling the Lottery. He was jailed for a year after presenting two halves of a torn ticket, claiming it had been ripped in half by his dog.

A banned driver

A twenty-three year old man bought a Mercedes with an Instants payout of £25,000 and promptly had it confiscated by the court. He had boasted in the press about getting the car despite being banned from driving. Police booked him when he took it out for a drive.

Husband of a practical joker

A man became ecstatic when he thought he had won £22 million after watching his numbers come up live on television. Fifteen minutes later his 'practical joker' wife announced that he had been watching a video of an earlier draw and she had filled out his ticket accordingly. The husband's official reaction was that it had been a 'great joke!'

An old soldier An old soldier went out drinking in January 1995 to celebrate a £200 win. After sinking twenty pints he was mugged and the rest of his cash stolen. He was arrested and thrown into a cell. He was later fined £30 for being drunk on a highway.

A winning family As they went to collect their winnings they were burgled and many irreplaceable items of sentimental value were stolen.

A young lady A young lady missed out on winning the jackpot on a Saturday in April by one second. The Lottery machine shut down on the 7.30pm deadline just as her winning numbers were being processed. The ticket would have won her £8.5 million. Camelot said, 'This is a most unfortunate case.' The girl's mother said, 'To lose like this is incredibly sad.' The young lady's response is not quotable!

A young man A twenty-seven-year-old man bought a ticket with the same numbers for seventeen weeks in a row. He then forgot to buy a ticket and his numbers came up. He would have won £2 million.

A relative of the Queen After losing a six-figure sum at Lloyds – at one stage she claimed she was so hard up she couldn't even afford to put petrol in her car – this lady admits she has become 'obsessive' about playing the National Lottery. 'Each week I'm convinced I'm going to win. I see it as the only way out of my financial problems. I do it because I lost absolutely everything through Lloyds. There was a time when I didn't go shopping for three months because I hadn't any money – my brother sent me pheasants and home-grown vegetables from the estate.' Each week she chooses her random numbers with the help of both a Lottery pen and keyring. 'I'm rather a child when it comes to doing the Lottery; it's the high spot of my week.'

Bookmakers	Ladbrokes cut 200 jobs in August 1995.
Gordon Kennedy	Shot from relative obscurity to co-host the television programme with Anthea Turner before being unceremoniously cast back from whence he came.
A jobless family	A jobless family from Blackburn have run up £11,000 of debts trying to win the Lottery jackpot and in August 1995 they were still chasing their dream of fabulous wealth. The family, which has three children under the age of seven, were at the mercy of loan sharks, faced with imprisonment for non-payment of council tax and had sold all their most treasured possessions. They ploughed their benefit payments into it, pinning their hopes on a win. 'It's a living hell,' the husband said. 'The Lottery has taken over my life. The only way out is to win

the jackpot.' On average they were spending £100 of their £208 weekly benefit payments and had sold their car, hi-fi, satellite dish and even their children's toys to try and pay off debts. The man, who appeared on the BBC 2 Public Eye documentary *Lottery Fever*, admitted 'Our debts are getting worse. I'm cracking up and need help. But it's impossible to walk past a shop and not buy a card. I might get ten at one go. It's a thrill that takes away the feeling that life isn't worth living. At night I even dream about the winning numbers. I feel I'm doing it for my family. I've always wanted somewhere nice to live for the kids. This is how we'll do it.' On one occasion they spent money they had set aside for new shoes for their daughter on cards and on another occasion had to be given an emergency £25 food voucher to feed the family. They have, however, got themselves prepared for the big win. They have had a legal agreement set up showing how any money will be split. The man's sister-in-law, who had never gambled before the Lottery, said, 'the only reason I don't spend more on scratch cards is that I don't have the money. The second I know I've lost I want more. I can't see a way out. It's impossible to stop. We are all in a trap.'

Nearly all of us

The advertising campaigns have persuaded so many of us to buy tickets because we feel we have as much chance as the next person. In reality we are more likely to be struck by lightning. Experts say that the Lottery has turned us into a 'nation of miserable gamblers'. Psychiatrist Peter Avron said, 'The Lottery is a measure of the misery many of us feel. We all want to escape from our predicament and it is a mass search for the feel-good factor. People are scared to stop because if they do they are faced with how much cash they have lost'. Colleague Dr Mark Griffiths said, 'Since the National Lottery started we have become a nation of gamblers. Once people thought gambling was bad. Now it is acceptable.' For many of us where we live is a factor. Some Lottery outlets are in Post Offices and people drawing benefit are tempted to buy a ticket. If you live in a depressing tower block it must be tempting to ask 'Does life really have to be like this?' And having watched television and seen the glossy ads, and idyllic holiday locations we know that for many it isn't. For some it is the rum punch in Barbados and the Porsche in the garage. Just one bit of luck on the Lottery, we muse, and it could be me too.

Blur have recorded a song about the Lottery on their *Great Escape* album. It points out the hopelessness of the dreamers who buy a ticket to 'somewhereville' every week and who are equally doomed to rip it up at five past eight every Saturday night.

CHAPTER 5

THE NATIONAL LOTTERIES BOARD AND THE EFFECT ON CHARITIES

Many charities are probably right to be concerned about their future income levels. The experience from the Irish Republic indicates that since the introduction of their national lottery in 1987 (which is played by an estimated 62% of the adult population spending on average £2.75 per person, per week) there has been a 50% fall off in charitable giving. The National Council of Voluntary Organisations (NCVO) also estimates that about 50% of Irish Lottery proceeds have substituted government spending. On top of this the Charities Aid Foundation has charted a gentle decline in giving in Britain since the high point of £18 billion was achieved in 1986. The figure has dropped to below £16 billion (average of eight out of ten adults giving £2.50 a month) before the National Lottery started. It is with this steady decline as a back-drop, together with ever-increasing demands on their money, that charities are particularly worried about the effects the National Lottery will have on their income. This is compounded by the fact that there are about 4000 new charities launched each year, creating what the *Daily Telegraph* described as 'a pond of spawning fish with the water level dropping.'

Research carried out by National Opinion Polls for the NCVO also found:

- The percentage of the population giving to charity since the Lottery began in November 1994 fell from 81% to 67%.

- The proportion of people buying raffle tickets fell from 32% to 17% while the percentage giving to street collections is down nearly one third to 23%.

- Total individual donations have dropped by some £71 million.

- They calculated that if the same pattern continued until the time of the National Lottery's first birthday (the survey was conducted in March 1995) charities and voluntary organisations could lose £212 million which would be £57 million more than it calculated the National Lottery Charities Board will have to distribute. In fact the shortfall was £41 million.

- Two out of three of those questioned thought that for every pound spent on the Lottery 22p went to charity, whereas the actual figure is a quarter of that (5.6p). This prompted Camelot to remove reference to charities in its advertising campaigns.

- NCVO worried from the outset that people may buy Lottery tickets in the belief that they are helping good causes yet that the money would be directed to projects they did not regard as worthwhile. Only one in ten of those surveyed, for example, would call building an Olympic stadium in Britain a 'very good cause' whilst 85% considered that services to elderly and disabled people would come into that category.

A survey of 20,000 *Sun* readers indicated that they would like to see the money distributed in the following ways:

Hospitals	50%
Medical research	36%
Children	13%
Education	10%

| Old people | 9% |
| Homeless/poor | 9% |

Sport came in at 1% and the Arts failed to make it at all.

There were very early indicators too that charities were particularly hard hit in the first few months of operation of the National Lottery. Voluntary Services Overseas saw a 10-15% drop in income and Arthritis Care saw income from its pre-Christmas lottery drop by 25%. Their fund-raising director, Peter Maple, said, 'Contrary to the Government's hope that the Lottery would generate extra income, at best we are going to recover our losses and at worst we've got a big hole in funding.'

Some charities were also fearful of a 'double whammy' as news leaked out to the Association of Medical Research Charities that despite the fact that their fund-raising was being affected they were going to be treated as low priority in the first rounds of charitable grant-making. In fact, there was so much adverse public reaction to this news that with some gentle Government persuasion they were eventually added to the list for allocation. This was not, however, in time for leading cancer research charity, Tenovus, which had to lose its nationwide scratch card scheme as a result of competition from the National Lottery. This cost the charity £1.5 million in a full year or half of its annual funding. In the previous fifteen years their lottery had raised £10 million and had helped to fund research and drug development as well as setting up advice and counselling centres. Tenovus called on the Government to provide compensation but this was not forthcoming.

However, despite the experience of Tenovus some lotteries have been quick to jump on the popularity bandwagon for both lottery and scratch cards. Since the introduction of the National Lottery, UK Charity Lotteries, the largest operator of scratch cards in the UK apart from the National Lottery, has seen its sales increase five-fold. A number of new charity scratch card operations have been successfully launched. The

Cancer Research Campaign, for example, saw an increase of 23% in its income in the last five months of the year despite the competition from the National Lottery. The Royal British Legion also marked its annual Poppy Appeal with a nationwide laser show and a £100,000 instant lottery card. The RBL will receive 20% of the takings of the cards which are operated by Lord Mancroft's Scratch 'n' Win company. Pat Reger, Secretary of the RBL Poppy Appeal is quite optimistic about the impact of spontaneous fund-raising and says, 'If anything it is stimulating us to take stock of our fund-raising strengths.' During the previous twelve years the amount raised had risen from £6 million to £15 million. It will be difficult to gauge the impact for the figure raised from 1995, however, because the impact of the 50th Anniversary of VE and VJ Days will have to be taken into consideration.

David Rigg, Camelot's Director of Communications, speaking at a Charities Aid Foundation conference, said that 'the jury was still out' on the Lottery's long-term impact but some charities had suffered and they 'suffered precisely at the same time as the National Lottery started'. However, he referred to an independent report that showed that charitable income as a whole across a broad base of charities had actually risen by 2.3% in the period April to June 1995 compared with the corresponding period for the previous year. What was perhaps more telling in the breakdown of that figure was that charities which actually used lotteries as a form of fund-raising had seen their incomes from that particular source increase by 71.3%.

One former fund-raiser also felt that charities were overstating their hand in their criticism of the National Lottery. In a letter to the *Daily Telegraph* in October 1995 Colonel Philip Howes wrote, 'As a former fund-raiser of a national charity for seven years I suspect that some charities are making far too much of the impact of the National Lottery on their fund-raising operations. Any adverse effect must be limited and confined to only one of the five main ways of giving to charity. Four methods cannot have been affected to any serious extent. These are grant-making trusts which recycle money that is already in the charitable sector, legacies, planned giving whether by covenant entered into over a period of years, payroll giving or through one-off Gift Aid, in which the tax aspect usually forms part of the donor's calculation. Lastly, there are events which rely on a major investment of time or money by already committed supporters. The exception is impulse giving – can clanking, inertia raffles and deposited envelopes. But any charity which relies too heavily on this one area should have sought to diversify its fund-raising operations sooner. No one can have failed to notice the advance publicity for the National Lottery. Charities must therefore look elsewhere for why their donations are declining.'

Despite different opinions it was still clear that many charities were really struggling. As a result of this, help was provided by the Charities Aid Foundation which launched a new magazine Lottery – the magazine for grant-seekers. The magazine is specifically designed to be user-friendly and help organisations maximise their opportunities for receiving money. It thus includes details of all available information about Lottery awards, any change in procedure, and case studies of organisations that succeeded with their applications.

But the news many charities wanted to hear came in November 1995 when the Government announced it is to closely monitor the effect of the National Lottery on donations to charity. Home Office officials said they were commissioning research to establish whether charities' income had actually fallen. Charities welcomed the move saying it was in response to 'widespread concerns.'

Stuart Etherington, the Chief Executive of the NCVO said, 'Our research on individual giving has suggested that fund-raising charities are losing public donations, particularly raffles, street collections and door-to-door collections since the start of the National Lottery'. The Home Office, which has responsibility for regulating charities said ministers were honouring a commitment given during the passage of the National Lottery Bill. Baroness Blatch, the Home Office Minister, said, 'The Government believed then, and still believes, that the National Lottery will be a significant new source of funding for charities.' She went on to say that the early evidence was 'very mixed' as to whether there had been a significant effect on charity income. The research is intended to look at all the main sources of charitable income – such as trading, donations and legacies – and will monitor changes in each since the introduction of the Lottery.

This has been done partly to help deflect criticism of where the first grants were given. Out of 4,500 applications 627 smaller charities actually shared in the first allocation of £40 million several months before any major awards were made to national charities. Whilst Mrs Bottomley publicly said that she was tired of people constantly 'whinging' about where the money was going she was also determined that medical and family charities were given priority. She indicated that more doctors might be appointed to the Charities Board which might also have to report to her rather than the Home Office. She added that as the Lottery giving unfolded 'we must be sure that all groups are benefiting and if there are any areas where we can modify it then I will be one of the first to encourage distributing bodies to take steps where there could be an improvement.'

Conscious of public criticism of multi-million pound Lottery awards to cultural institutions the Charities Board made their initial grants relatively small and allocated them to small community-based groups. A Board spokesman indicated that those looking for larger grants would have to wait longer.

However, despite this change of tactic the decisions attracted significant criticism as some newspapers 'cherry picked' groups they would attack. One main grouping which received such treatment was ethnic minority organisations. The Eritrean Advice and Information Centre based in South London received £90,000 to help immigrants living in Britain deal with benefit claims. A Charities Board spokesman described their application as 'water-tight', adding that the award was good value for money and 'would help them become self-sufficient, not a drain on the country.' Others in this category to receive flack were the Vietnamese Mental Health Project (£174,000), an Afro-Caribbean association and a Chinese Women's group in Gloucestershire. David Mellor, the former Heritage Secretary, complained that these grants were made solely on the grounds of 'political correctness'. He described the Board as a 'creaky old tub...piled full of some of the usual suspects of politically correct vehicles' which had been 'permitted to go its own way'. Mr Sieff described the attack as 'nonsense' saying that they had surveyed nearly 8,000 voluntary organisations to learn their views and identify their priorities.

The Vietnamese Mental Health Project run by Dr Cam in Brixton also does worthwhile work. He and his seven staff help prevent psychiatric misdiagnosis through cultural misunderstandings and provide back-up for 200 mentally ill men and women among London's 17,000-strong Vietnamese community. Memories of executions, the destruction of their homes, prison and torture have left a catalogue of trauma that requires treatment. The project has a permanent home for six mentally ill people where they are taught self-reliance.

The Chinese women's group in Gloucester received £7,000, part of which will be spent on an interpreter to assist with things such as shopping. Mew Ming Chan Edmead, their Chairman, said its work was vital to the estimated 2000 Chinese living in the county.

The biggest grant awarded, £666,117 to the Strathclyde Poverty Alliance, also received criticism from Mr Mellor as well as from Phil Gallie, Conservative MP for Ayr, who said that the funds would have been better allocated to 'organisations like the Royal National Institute for the Blind who are doing good work in Scotland' instead of groups like the SPA which they claimed were concerned with single party politics. But John Rafferty, the Board's director in Scotland, said the award was 'right and justified' and that the Tory party comments, made because the SPA campaigns on issues such as restoration of benefits for 16-18 year olds and cold weather payments, were incomprehensible. He insisted that the SPA, which provides training for local community groups seeking to combat poverty in the west of Scotland, was a genuine charity and thus not a political organisation. Saying that the SPA did very valuable work, he added that the Scottish Office itself provided £33,000 for one of their projects. The director of SPA, Damian Killeen, called the criticism 'ill-informed' and said that political campaigns and lobbying represented only a very small part of their work. It was impossible, he said, to avoid being accused of political bias when dealing with issues like poverty. The vast bulk of the SPA's work is with members of its 500 affiliated community groups in the Glasgow area. The alliance provides training and skills programmes for people to enable them to lobby their local authorities and health boards. It has also helped groups to set up food co-operatives, credit unions and transport services in a region where three out of ten families are on Income Support.

David Sieff, who at the same time had to respond to the criticisms regarding spending £1.26 million on consultancy fees, was particularly unhappy about some of the media criticism the awards generated. He said, 'These journalists seem to believe their readers would rather step over the corpses of the victims of drug abuse, HIV illness, refugees from overseas and those unable to afford shelter.'

The initial top ten awards

1. **Strathclyde Poverty Alliance, Scotland.** To equip and support community activists to combat poverty locally, £666,117.
2. **Yorkhill Family House Limited, Scotland.** To provide free accommodation for the families of sick children, £635,000.
3. **Inverclyde Community Development Trust, Scotland.** Relief of poverty by providing premises for new business development, £626,096.
4. **The Social Iceberg Foundation, Scotland.** Building on current work to provide innovative experimental integrated service, £555,000.

5. **All Women Centre, Scotland.** To support women in all areas of multiple deprivation, £470,347.
6. **Voluntary Service, Aberdeen, Scotland.** Alleviating poverty and developing positive approaches to overcoming it, £458,455.
7. **Merkinch Enterprise Limited, Scotland.** Merkinch enterprise residents' Action on Poverty Programme, £413,350.
8. **West Whitlawburn Housing Cooperative Limited, Scotland.** To arrest the social and economic decay of a deprived community, £400,055.
9. **Lothian and Edinburgh Environmental Partnership, Edinburgh.** Energy and fuel advice for Edinburgh's poor, £384,500.
10. **Cumbernauld YMCA, Scotland.** To establish, test and evaluate a Cumbernauld area foyer service, £382,500.

All the above are Scottish and 44% of the first distribution's total went there. This is purely because the Scottish arm made faster progress in assessing bids. England caught up in the following months.

The initial smallest awards

1. **Clych Cledwyn, Wales.** Clych Cledwyn Pre-school development and activity centre, £882.
2. **The Management Committee of West Lothian Scout Association, Scotland.** Entrance road to the West Lothian Scout Training Centre, £880.
3. **Burton Mother and Toddler Group, SW England.** A safe floor for the Burton mother and toddler group, £864.
4. **103rd Leeds (St Wilfrid's) Guide Company, Yorks and Humberside.** Offer reprieve from local pressures, promote self-belief, £750.
5. **Whitburn Centre Playgroup, Scotland.** Whitburn Centre Playgroup – learn and play safe and secure, £615.
6. **Gallowhill Elderly Forum, Scotland.** For ongoing work for the elderly, £600.

7. **St Luke's Family Centre, Northern Ireland.** Creche and tutors' costs for parents' group, £522.
8. **Phoenix Toy Library, SW England.** To buy multicultural and equal opportunities toys and instruments, £500.
9. **Ysgol Fethrin Y Felinheli, Wales.** Install safety flooring surface on play area, £500.
10. **Clych Meithrin Carmel, Wales.** To purchase equipment for Carmel Playgroup, £500.

Of the original grants about 25% went to groups working with children. Household names among recipients included Citizens Advice Bureaux (£1.9 million), the Royal National Institute for the Blind (£188,500) and Scope, formerly the Spastics Society (£315,000). The Board, however, primarily concentrated on helping smaller community-based projects with nearly half of the grants going to organisations with an annual turnover of less than £20,000. Typical recipients therefore included the Hull Council of Disabled People (£59,000 for a transport scheme) and the 19th Swindon Scout Group (£1,480 for minibus equipment).

In response to criticisms as to where the money went it was pointed out that only 6% went to ethnic minority groups, 3% to charities dealing with drug and alcohol addiction and under 1% to refugee groups. Stuart Etherington, the NCVO chief executive, was supportive of the distribution but implored the Government to increase the percentage of money allocated to charities as only 14% of applicants had been successful. Jack Cunningham, the Shadow National Heritage Secretary, also backed the distribution. Referring to outraged attacks from certain parts of the press he said he was 'appalled by the tone of those stories' and he went on to praise the way in which money had been given to small local groups and spread well around the country.

To deflect criticism the National Lotteries Charities Board also produced a rolling programme showing how each batch of grants was going to be prioritised. The initial period looked as follows:

Autumn 1995	people living in poverty.
Spring 1996	health, disability, medical research, small grants and UK charities abroad.
Summer 1996	new opportunities and choices.
Winter 1996	improving people's living environment.
Spring 1997	community involvement.

Regional distribution

Regional distribution, although on the whole well received, received some criticism. One regional paper complained that Greater London received almost 25% of the initial payout and that meant that London received nearly £21 per head as compared with Yorkshire £10 and the East Midlands £3.50. Needless to say, London saw it differently! Steve Wyler, director of London Voluntary Service Council, was concerned that London was actually missing out because 'poverty is far worse there than anywhere else'.

Given that it is easier to be negative than positive and thus criticise what is happening elsewhere it would appear that the distribution was about right. Certainly there was far less criticism of the second distribution either in terms of regional bias or in the actual distribution which involved such well-known names as the Samaritans, Mencap, The Scouts and Guides, and St John's Ambulance.

Some charities that lost

Many large charities come into this category. As previously mentioned, **Tenovus** has been one of the main casualties with nearly half its funding threatened when it had to withdraw its own lottery, but there have been others as well. The National Lottery was partly blamed for the closure of the Royal National Institute for the Blind's Sunshine House School at East Grinstead. Their director of education, Paul Ennals, blamed a deficit of £2.5 million on a drop in legacy income and the 'adverse effect' of the National Lottery on some of its fund-raising. Mr Ennals claimed that they therefore had no option but to close the school and move the pupils to other RNIB schools.

Age Concern also suffered. Frank Ecclestone, chairman of Age Concern Lincoln, wrote in their monthly newsletter 'Monthly Link', 'Over the past two years we have experienced a fall-off in income and this is due in the main to the coming of the National Lottery which is siphoning off a very large percentage of available money normally donated to charity. People are excited by the hope of winning millions of pounds and dreams of how they are going to spend it. Raising money for our association is not easy.'

Perhaps most worrying of all was an announcement in December 1995 that **Save the Children** – one of Britain's largest charities – had been forced to make sweeping cuts of £9 million to its projects across the world because of a continuing fall in income which was, it says, compounded by the effects of the National Lottery. The charity, which funds projects in fifty countries and has the Princess Royal as its president, is to cut its annual overall budget of £91 million by 10% before April 1997. Don Redding, a spokesman for the charity said, 'It's a very tough fund-raising climate anyway and half our income is from voluntary contributions so when you add the Lottery to that it's a significant new pressure that adds to the problems. The cuts will lead to job losses and the closure of projects including family centres and schemes for young people leaving care in Britain. In the changed world of the nineties we have found ourselves trapped between massively rising demands around the world as children become poorer and a recession which has affected everyone's pocket at home.' Camelot said they hoped that in the long-term Save the Children would benefit substantially from Lottery funding and pointed out that they had already received £379,000 for a scheme working with children on an estate in Rochdale.

There is, of course, another group of charities that do not benefit and they are those who choose not to apply for funding. This can be for moral or ethical or religious reasons. For example, gambling is frowned upon by Muslims. It may be that others are opposed to seeking funding from the Lottery because they are concerned about the negative impact it could be argued it is having upon our society and I believe that this is where most of the Christian denominations are coming from. It could be that some charities who are involved in debt counselling and helping people with gambling problems refuse to apply on the grounds that they think it would be hypocritical to apply to the Lottery for funding when they see it as being partly responsible for the problems they are trying to solve. As a Christian money education charity I think you can clearly see where this leaves Credit Action! However, if these charities' supporters do not maintain their level of giving the charities concerned will inevitably suffer.

Some charities that won

Again there are many in this category so I thought it would be easiest to highlight a few to show just a glimpse of where the money is going.

Ormiston Trust, Newmarket – This charity is based at a

former pub and was set up to help children and families. They were awarded £105,000 which will be used for a new cooker and other kitchen equipment, as well as allowing more time to be allocated to counselling for families with financial problems. Director, Sue Blake, said that much of the cash would go towards re-equipping the kitchen to provide regular meals for preschool children. 'The grant will mean that we can sustain this work for the next two years,' she said. Up to seventy families make use of the centre every week.

Ely Victim Support Scheme – They were awarded £15,150 for their basic work and an additional £20,000 for a special rural volunteer bureau for people 'facing isolation'. This will provide a gardening and decorating scheme and the extra cash will help fund a part-time co-ordinator, new equipment and a move to more central premises.

Emmaus – three years ago Emmaus was a fledgling charity based in Landbeach, Cambridgeshire, but since then it has grown rapidly opening other communities in Coventry, Greenwich and Dover with plans to open five more. The grant of £299,000 will help support the expansion of existing communities and the launch of new ones. The Emmaus Movement was started by a French priest, Abbé Pierre, in post-war France. Its aim is to help the homeless help themselves. Abbé Pierre would take homeless people back to his presbytery where he encouraged them to recycle and sell things that other people had thrown away. There are now some 360 communities worldwide. The Landbeach community has a thriving recycling business and shop. Each community offers a home, work, independence from state benefit, companionship and renewed self-respect for homeless people. Their national director, Iain Mackechnie-Jarvis, believes there could be as many as 350,000 people who are homeless in Britain. He had been concerned that they were unable to help many groups who had contacted them wanting to start their own communities so he sees getting the Lottery money as a 'remarkable turnaround'.

BESS – The Benchill Ecumenical Service Scheme based

on a large council estate in south Manchester was awarded £97,000. The project was formed by local Anglican, Catholic and Methodist churches and there had been some anguished debate about whether money should be sought from the Lottery, particularly among the Methodists who traditionally have a distaste for gambling. The project was set up eight years ago to offer support, counselling and music and drama experiences to residents in an area of high unemployment and social deprivation. They have four support workers, two of whom work principally with young families. The Lottery money will help develop a family support centre set up at the Methodist church a year ago. It is open five days a week providing a play group, mother and toddler group, clothing shop and credit union. 'We're delighted,' said Sue Jenkins of BESS. 'The residents of Benchill had no real voice and were not being heard. The vision of BESS was to raise their very low self-esteem and develop the skills and confidence of local people through music and drama.'

LASER – The Liverpool Accessible Sensory Environment Resource group received £150,000. Kevin Cowdall of LASER had no qualms about applying to the Lottery. 'You have to look at it objectively,' he said. 'You have to treat it like any other fund-raising trust, admittedly the biggest in Europe. You have to look at the criteria which this time were geared towards poverty and grass roots organisations. We fitted those criteria.' Mr Cowdall estimated that 95% of LASER's potential client group would be Lottery players. He said he will look to City Challenge and other sources to fund the balance of an admittedly ambitious scheme to convert the Owenite Hall of Science in Liverpool into a centre providing therapy, play, education and stimulation for children with disabilities. At its heart will be a sensory stimulation room, hence the project's incredible title!

Conclusion

What is clear is that a significant number of charitable donations will be lost for ever. Even though more people realise that charities have actually suffered because of the National Lottery, they are still in the minority. Small change that would go into a shopkeeper's charity tin now buys a scratch card. But in turn this does mean that many charities have to become more focused – look at their costings, get clearer direction and target the people and organisations that could well be interested in supporting them. It could well be a difficult few years but it could be argued that the advent of the National Lottery has actually accelerated a move that was much needed in any case.

CHAPTER 6

THE OTHER BODIES

The Arts Council

The Arts Council has received considerable criticism for the way in which it has allocated funds. The biggest protest was undoubtedly aimed at the £78 million pounds awarded to the Royal Opera House. This, not surprisingly, prompted complaints that this was a classic example of the Lottery being a 'tax on the poor to benefit the rich', especially as the Arts Council is a co-owner of the Royal Opera House! Hardly had the dust settled there, however, when another major London arts institution, The Royal Court Theatre, benefited to the tune of £16 million. Its artistic director, Stephen Daldry, claimed that the country's foremost home for new playwrights would have had to close without the money. He said, 'The theatre is in such a terrible state that without this funding we would not have been able to survive more than about eighteen months. This would have meant the end of this unique and wonderful playhouse. Now we can face the future with confidence and carry on the work of promoting new plays and playwrights.' The grant will go towards a £21 million development which will be finished in about three years and provide better seating and a restaurant under Sloane Square. Backstage facilities will be improved and the theatre's back wall, which was in danger of collapsing, will be made safe. Some critics, however, would have liked to have seen the whole theatre fall down – not just the back wall. One arts correspondent claimed that Lottery ticket buyers had saved a theatre which put on a 'disgusting feast of filth'. He particularly complained about the play *Blasted* which had such uplifting features as rape, torture, cannibalism and a dead baby.

Everything was not so controversial however. Lord Gowrie, the Arts Council chairman and noted film fanatic, made his mark with several grants to the film industry. About £12.3 million was put aside to help finance six movies. The biggest grant was towards the total £4 million cost of Thomas Hardy's *The Woodlanders* with the rest of the money being provided by Channel 4. Again in order to deflect criticism the Arts Council will retain the right to veto casting on all the film projects that are partially funded from Lottery money and will insist on largely British actors. Lord Gowrie said, 'We are particularly pleased that the first three features are by directors who have shown considerable promise in the areas of film-making', adding that the usual insistence on partnership funding of 25% from the private sector had been increased to 50% because of the high level of risk inherent in the film business. 'Funding the British film industry is very much a part of our remit,' Lord Gowrie said as the Arts Council announced awards totalling just under £30 million and also plans to put up to £75 million into films in the next five years. He said, 'If we can provide a bit of venture capital, money comes in. The risks are high and whether a film is going to get a return is an impossible thing to predict. Even the very efficient industry in Hollywood can't do that.'

A centre for celebrating popular music from 17th century opera to rock and roll will also be able to be established in Sheffield aided by £1.5 million from Lottery funds. This centre is expected to attract half a million visitors a year and will contain exhibits and archives, documenting popular music and its surrounding culture. It will be only the second project of its kind in the world – the Rock and Roll Hall of Fame opened in Cleveland, Ohio in September 1995.

There has been a wide range of awards and the samples below show their diverse nature:

Avonbank Brass Band – £22,000 towards instruments
Crouch End Clock Tower Centenary Celebration
   Committee – £1,400 towards seating and railings
The Folly Trust, Lancaster – £94,415 towards a photo-
   graphic and video centre
Montford Handbell Ringers – £5,300 towards a set of
   bells

In October 1995 the Arts Council awarded £30 million to Sadler's Wells to pull down its building in Rosebey Avenue, North London and replace it with 'the most futuristic theatre in Britain.' The Council backed the glass and steel multi-art theatre which will have the largest stage in London because it is intended to put London back on the international dance touring circuit. The original 1683 Sadler's Wells will be re-erected in the foyer before its expected opening in 1998.

After spending so much money in London the Council started to go some way towards redressing the balance. Major awards were made to the National Glass Centre in Sunderland (£5.9 million) and the Manchester Contact Theatre (£4.5 million).

At the Arts Council Annual General Meeting in Autumn 1995 Lord Gowrie said the National Lottery is 'little less than a revolution' which is transforming Britain's cultural landscape. But although saying that Lottery funds are starting to make a huge impact on investment in the arts he warned that current funding was still tight given the cut in real terms of 12% in the Government grant in the past two years. At the meeting Clive Priestley, chairman of the London Arts Board, warned there was a danger that the Lottery was creating a paradox of 'capital riches and revenue rags.' The reason for this is that one condition of eligibility for Lottery money was that the application has to be for a capital rather than a revenue project – indications are that this is now to be changed.

Following this constructive criticism Lord Gowrie himself suggested that Lottery money be used to commission new plays for theatres. Using the money for commissioning new work – and of course this would apply to operas and symphonies as well as plays – would delight the arts world but would cause hostile comment from those who would see it as a further example of money being used for elitist and minority tastes.

One of the problems the arts world has had to face is that government spending on the arts had been cut and was trimmed again by 3% in the 1995 budget. The Arts Council had clung to the hope that funding would remain unchanged in the light of John Major's pledge that 'the money raised by the Lottery will not replace existing government spending'. In the event, however, the budget was cut by £5 million, a reduction in real terms of more than 6%. Lord Gowrie reacted forthrightly to this 'broken promise' and refused to carry out his legal duty to distribute the Council's grants to the nation's arts organisations until mid-January 1996.

The boost to the arts that the National Lottery has brought is already causing problems and there is a real danger that the blurring of lines between Lottery and Government funding will increase. If the Lottery is seen as the main paymaster of the arts then Government grants are likely to keep reducing and this of course spells real danger to arts groups who do not put in Lottery bids perhaps because they have revenue but not capital requirements. As we will see later in this chapter, the Government has made the same reductions in national heritage funding. The problem is that the more capital projects that are supported by the National Lottery the greater will be the demands on the Arts Council to pay to keep them open. As politicians of all parties regard the arts as a low priority for spending so the gap between demand for subsidy and the State's willingness to provide it is likely to grow increasingly wider and it must therefore become essential that in one form or other decent revenue funding is found.

The Millennium Commission

The main criticism that has been levelled at the Commission is that rather than looking at ways to mark the turn of the Millennium itself it simply waits for ideas to come to it and then accepts or rejects them. Critics say that a nationally planned proactive campaign would be much more worthwhile. The transformation of the dilapidated and semi-derelict Bankside Power Station in London into a new Tate Gallery with a grant of £50 million was one of the first major awards. Not much opposition, other than 'London again', was heard about this partly because the defunct power station has been staring forlornly over the Thames for more than a decade now. The aim of transforming it into the centre-piece of an arts quarter that will do for Southwark what the Pompidou Centre did for the once decaying Beaubourg area of Paris is inspiring. Jeremy Fraser, the leader of Southwark Council, actually took the Millennium Commissioners to the top of the power station which will become the highest public observation platform in London. 'This is regeneration', said Mr Fraser, adding that he believed it would change the focal point of the city. Nicholas Serota, the Tate's director, said, 'It will do an extraordinary amount to help Londoners rediscover the Thames.' The new Tate should prove to be the catalyst for redevelopment along the South Bank. With local unemployment running at about 25% Southwark Council has extracted commitments that construction workers will be recruited locally and that all jobs in the new gallery will be offered first in the borough. Some 650 jobs are expected to be thus created in the community and 2,400 across London as a whole.

Other major awards have included a programme for regenerating Portsmouth Harbour at a cost of £40 million. This scheme focuses on the creation of an international maritime leisure complex and should create several hundred construction jobs and up to 3,500 permanent jobs on completion. A 165 ft high observation tower and a series of water jets that will be fired over ferries and ships as they enter the harbour will be big features. The chairman of the Portsmouth project, Ben Stoneham, believes the finished project will be as significant to Britain as Sydney Opera House is to Australia.

The Earth Centre in Doncaster was also given a large grant of £50 million. It will be a state of the art centre for environmental research and sustainable technology on a 350 acre site that was formerly home to two deep mine collieries. At its heart will be an environmentally friendly building, the Ark, designed as a large exhibition and activities space on three levels connected by moving walkways. The Commission also granted £5.75 million as the first stage 'to change the face of Scotland' by planting billions of trees across forty-five different woodland projects to help create a Millennium Forest in Scotland. Another worthwhile grant in Scotland was £7.5 million to put the collections of over 200 Scottish museums on CD-ROM which would be accessible to every school.

One very popular award was £12 million to restore the Rochdale Canal. The restoration project is staggering as it involves ninety-one locks over thirty-two miles which in the 19th century would have taken even the fastest narrowboat more than a week to complete. John Battye, leader of Oldham Council, said 'We have worked for almost a decade with government agencies and the voluntary sector to transform long stretches of this once neglected canal into an attractive park well used by the local people and visitors alike.' The Lottery cash will mean that remaining blockages to navigation can be removed thus enabling a complete 'Pennine ring' for canal users as it will link up with the Leeds-Liverpool canal.

Awards that were announced just prior to Christmas 1995 continued to attract controversy. The largest donation was £21.5 million to Kew Gardens to help them establish a new seed bank on a six acre site at Wakehurst Place, Sussex. Researchers at Kew said that the grant had come 'just in the nick of time' as some experts had forecast up to 25% of worldwide plant species becoming extinct in the next fifty years unless urgent action is taken now. The new seed bank will be a safe haven for at least 10% of the world's flora by 2010.

The 'black beaches' of Durham, polluted by a century of spoil-tipping from the county's once extensive coal industry, received a grant of £4.5 million so that they can be cleared to form a nature reserve. David Bellamy described the area as a 'special place for lovers of nature.'

But once again complaints were heard, particularly of 'London bias' when the Millennium Fund refused a proposed £50 million grant for the Cardiff Bay Opera House. However, the opera buff's loss could be the rugby spectator's gain as the Welsh Rugby Union is applying for £55 million to help rebuild their national stadium ahead of the 1999 World Cup and there was little likelihood that both would be approved. This was confirmed in March 1996.

Virginia Bottomley, the Heritage Secretary, claims the Commission has also sketched out how individuals might win new millennium bursaries from Lottery funds which have so far only been devoted to capital projects. The awards, which would be on offer to people of all ages, would not be 'primarily about an individual furthering his or her intellectual skills or economic capacity but would be linked to wider community benefits and fellowship'. She suggested that the awards might reflect individuals' contributions to communities, the environment and science and technology. She also envisaged they might cover the arts, sports and heritage if public consultation backed the idea. The plans were that they would be funded at first through annual Lottery income but later through a £100 million investment fund. Even though hundreds, if not thousands, of awards are expected by the year 2000 they do not appear to fully respond to Labour's call for a Lottery 'talent fund' which would help young athletes, musicians, artists, designers and engineers.

The National Heritage Memorial Fund

Just like the arts the NHMF suffered a £4 million cut in Government funding last year and faces another reduction of £800,000 in 1996/7 to reduce it to just £8 million per annum. The Lottery must obviously 'take the blame' here – the Treasury surely arguing the merits of bolstering the Fund with money which is badly needed elsewhere when the Lottery is giving it £300 million a year anyway? This was highlighted in a letter to *The Times* in October 1995 from Dr Neil Chalmers, director of the National History Museum. In it he wrote, 'There has been a decline in real terms in the grant-in-aid that the Natural History Museum, among others, has experienced in recent years.... Given that museums and galleries are vital to one of the few growth areas of Britain, namely leisure and tourism, this policy goes directly against the Government's intention to increase wealth generation and improve the quality of life. The link between the arrival of the Lottery and the decline in government funding seems to me to be inescapable. The Lottery is being used to replace government funding by the back door.'

The danger with this argument is that the Lottery fund is looking at a more populist agenda – particularly after the initial public relations disaster when purchasing the Churchill Papers for £12.5 million. Using Lottery money to save works of art from export goes down badly in the popular press as it is paying rich people with poor people's money. Many consider that the government has a duty to provide some money of its own to prevent national treasures from being sold abroad.

That the Heritage Fund is now using Lottery money for more populist causes can be clearly seen from the group of projects it is currently supporting. These include Croome Park where the National Trust has been given £4.9 million to buy what is probably Capability Brown's most influential creation. The Trust said that the 675 acre park near Worcester was 'one of the great creative works of the 18th century.' It remains virtually intact and will be opened to the public when some restoration work has been completed. 'This was Capability Brown's first great landscape park and it is of tremendous importance,' said David Brown, the National Trust's regional public relations manager. 'It is probably the birthplace of Britain's modern love affair with gardening.'

A grant of £3 million was awarded to help fund the Thackray Medical Museum in Leeds. Housed in a former workhouse, the museum will incorporate a comprehensive exhibition of historical medical equipment as well as an educational department for medical students. Up to 200,000 visitors a year are expected.

The fact that the National Heritage Fund is being swamped with Lottery money has brought a further dilemma to the Church. Many Church of England churches, for example, would previously have applied to the Fund for money for restoration. To do so now means that they are in effect taking Lottery money and, in many cases, the Lottery is something they are strongly opposed to. Depending on one's point of view however, pragmatism, greed or lack of faith has generally won over principle, and churches are likely to be some of the major recipients of National Heritage funding. For example, many small grants have already been given for bells, organs and rebuilding and Bath Abbey has received £500,000 to help clean its interior. The rector of Bath Abbey, Prebendary Richard Askew, said 'I regard the introduction of the Lottery as a fresh form of gambling which slips us down the road of materialism a bit further. But it exists and this is how the Government has decided to fund Britain's heritage. We, who are the stewards, must face up to it and draw on funds so raised.'

During its first year of operation with Lottery funds the NHLF has given £70 million in grants. The breakdown is as follows:

26%   Land
17%   Buildings
24%   Museums and galleries
19%   Manuscripts

   14%   Industrial, maritime, transport

Despite a fairly even spread in grants the Fund got caught up
in controversy when it declared that a museum at Bletchley
Park, to celebrate the work of Britain's wartime code-break-
ers, would not be of interest to most people today and in any
case was too 'over-ambitious and under-developed.' The
response astounded the Bletchley Park Trust, which had the
support of John Major, because a feasibility study by the
Department of the Environment had found the viability of
the project to be sound. Like everywhere else the demands
and funds available do not tally.

The Sports Council

Pressure has also built up on the way the Sports Council allo-
cate their Lottery funding. For example, they have been
encouraged to make money available to help gifted teenagers
attend John Major's planned Academy of Sport. Both the
British Olympic Association and the British Athletic
Federation are among those who called on the Government
to allow Lottery money to be spent on coaching, sports med-
icine and science. David Carpenter, head of the Sports
Council National Lottery Unit, responded to these comments by saying that he was hopeful that this would happen
by mid-1996. As with other bodies this would relax the ruling that cash is only available for capital projects.

   There are other relaxations that sport would like to see
take place. Local councils have been angry that the Lottery
would fund only up to 65% of capital projects. They have
said that this means that richer councils with higher reserves
are more able to get Lottery money than those in areas where
it is often most badly needed. Paradoxically, and much to the
annoyance of the sports world, arts applications can be
funded up to 95% of their requirement.

   As well as this there have been claims that Lottery money
for sports facilities is merely hiding government-forced cuts
in council leisure budgets. This accusation, made in a report

by the Association of Metropolitan Authorities, revealed that whilst £115 million of Lottery money has been spent on capital projects, local councils have been forced to trim leisure budgets because they cannot afford some upkeep. The report highlights spending cuts that have been reflected in a spate of facility closures. Both Birmingham and Liverpool have had to close two swimming pools because they had no money to refurbish them. 'It appears that the Lottery is a sticking plaster hiding the cancer of the government's own creation,' said Chris Helnitz, chair of the leisure committee of the report's producers.

The breakdown of the first 130 awards made by the Sports Council is worth looking at, particularly as there appeared to be a dearth of applications from inner cities. This helps to explain why London received only seven of the grants. The distribution by sport was:

Cricket	23
Tennis	14
Football	12
Bowls	10
Rugby League	2
Boxing	2

Several swimming pools were also among the beneficiaries. This of course has led to claims that too much money is going to 'middle class' sports. The main grants given so far are:

Daventry District Council –
                    £5.7 million for a sport centre
Jubilee Sailing Trust –
                    £4.1 million for a sailing shop
Royal Albert Dock Trust –
                    £3.75 million for a watersports centre

Sail Training Association –
                        £3.5 million
Newcastle City Council –
                        £3.5 million for a swimming pool

At this stage at least some of the criticism levelled at the Sports Council does appear to be justified.

CHAPTER 7

GAMBLING SCHOOL? THE EFFECTS ON OUR CHILDREN

Even as the National Lottery began concern was being expressed as to the impact it would have on our children. Maggie Brown on 25 November 1994 wrote in the *Independent*, 'Consider for a moment the seductive impact on children of the Lottery – images of floating pound notes and the promise of instant painless wealth. Taking their cue from adults, children are already obsessed with how to get money and spend it.' The chairman of the National Council on Gambling wrote to *The Times* in January 1995 voicing his concerns. In part of the letter he wrote 'At present there is massive stimulation for demand for gambling and the promotion of the view that, rather than being a form of entertainment, it is a likely way of becoming rich. In this setting, although the controlled legislation prohibits children from purchasing Lottery tickets much of the publicity appears to be directed towards them. Thus children have been involved in the television commercials for the Lottery, and many children take part in the live audience at the time of the draw which in any case occurs before the 9 o'clock watershed.'

Since then a variety of sources have voiced their concern. For example, consultants wrote to the *British Medical Journal* urging that public education campaigns be launched to highlight the risks involved in gambling and that schools should be involved in this. They pointed out that an

Independent Television Commission survey had indicated that the weekly televised Lottery draw was the second most popular programme watched by 10-15 year olds [who are legally prohibited from buying tickets]. There has also been a proliferation of lottery-style game shows for children on television.

The Gaming Board made a recommendation in mid-1995 that sales of National Lottery tickets and instant scratch cards should be banned to children under eighteen. Their Annual Report said the age should be raised to bring it into line with the legal age for casino gambling, betting on horse races and bingo. They were particularly concerned about the impact of scratch cards which they referred to as 'a harder form of gambling'. Camelot defended sales to sixteen year olds. 'This is not about gambling but spending a couple of pounds on a flutter. Anyway it is the same age for the football pools.'

By late 1995 things were getting so bad that Oflot, the National Lottery watchdog, announced it was to publish a report on illegal sales of tickets to children following disclosure that they were regularly being sold to under-16s. They said they had carried out a survey in Devon which had shown that tickets were being regularly sold to children. It was out of such concern that the report was handed to the police. A Camelot spokesman said that it had not seen the results of the survey which showed that 50% of attempts to buy tickets by under-16s were successful. But it confirmed it would investigate and suspend any retailers who knowingly sold to that age group. They pointed out that they had recently removed a Lottery terminal from a retailer in Liverpool following an investigation into alleged sales to children. Devon's trading standards officer said that some retailers did not seem to be aware that youngsters had to be sixteen before they could buy a ticket, even though Camelot frequently reinforced the issue.

Another survey in north-west London showed that many thirteen-year-olds claimed to be sixteen or that their parents were waiting for them outside the shop. Many others in the

10-15 year bracket regularly asked their parents to buy them tickets. The survey also found one child who regularly spent all of her £10 pocket money on the Lottery each week. None of the children questioned had been asked to produce any ID. Potential future problems seem certain when a thirteen-year-old girl says that her father's frequent winning convinces her it is right to do the Lottery. 'I buy a scratch card each week and my dad gets me a Lottery ticket. I've never won but my dad always wins when he does it.' Ever since the Lottery began it has been a major topic of conversation at the school where the survey was carried out. 'If you win you talk about it, if you don't you shut up,' explained one girl neatly encapsulating the problems and experiences of many hidden gamblers.

These surveys and other anecdotal evidence also led to the National Council on Gambling giving even stronger warnings. Their chairman, Dr Emanuel Moran, who is also consultant psychiatrist at Grovelands Priory Hospital, argued that Lottery tickets and scratch cards should only be sold from licensed premises to reinforce the exclusion of children from gambling activities. Already, he said, the percentage of under-age Lottery players was near to mirroring the overall participation rate. The hype surrounding the weekly broadcasting of the draw, the widespread sale of tickets to those under age and the heavy promotion of scratch cards alongside the sweet counter in many shops could well lead to gambling dependence in later life for vulnerable children,' he believed. 'Society's consensus that gambling is an adult activity has been broken by the introduction of the National Lottery and the sale of tickets from ordinary retail outlets,' he said, adding that small regular payouts and huge publicity for the big winners had reinforced the gambling tendency. 'We are storing up problems for the future. My experience is that people who regularly played fruit machines (the only other form of gambling that is allowed outside licensed premises) as children are now presenting in their twenties with serious gambling problems. We are paying the price for that. The same danger applies to the Lottery.' He added, 'Addiction tends to develop over months or years and is driven by habit. The Lottery is less than two years old. In another year or two we could be seeing addiction among youngsters.' Scratch cards with their promise of immediate riches were a greater risk than the weekly Lottery draw for children because it would appear that they provide a 'quick fix'. Scratch cards have many of the features of hard gaming such as large instant jackpots and also 'heart-stoppers' which are cards that give the illusion that the person who bought the ticket has almost won a major prize because two large similar numbers actually did come up. This of course tempts people to try again because they feel either lucky or that they were almost there. Of course, this sort of pressure also applies to the purchase of Lottery tickets where 45% of players select the same numbers each week. The fear here is that 'it would just be my luck for these numbers to come up the week I didn't buy a ticket.' Incidentally, Camelot say that there are about 10,000 people each week who select the number 1-6 inclusive. This would mean that if the 14 million to one chance did actually happen these people would actually win a jackpot of approximately £800 each!

It is exactly this form of mindless gambling naiveté that Dr Moran is concerned about. He said, 'The availability and promotion of gambling facilities are important in the causation of pathological gambling. Before the introduction of the National Lottery public policy under successive governments, including the present one, allowed gambling only to the extent that was needed to meet unstimulated demand. However, the Lottery has been promoted vigorously and this has involved children.'

The pressures that any form of gambling can have on children also received comment from an unlikely source. The film maker Martin Scorsese, talking about Las Vegas, says, 'Where is it leading to? It's leading to...people who can't afford it, going there and losing their money – and bringing their kids. It's giving the children the wrong signal. It desensitises them. It seems all right because they see their parents losing money. I don't think it's a good idea to encourage people to think that all they have to do is [gamble] and all their troubles will be over.' Adults can make their own decisions, he argues, but there are consequences which for their children can be both damaging and lead to a wrong value system. This can be clearly seen when looking at queues at Lottery terminals. Many mums and dads have their children in tow, giving the impression that everything is fine and it is a normal part of adult living.

In November 1995 a fifteen-year-old from Scholar Green, Cheshire found himself in a quandary. Either the magic finger of the Lottery had pointed to him and he was suddenly £10,000 better off or he was penniless and facing a criminal record. The uncertainty arose after Camelot called in the police to investigate how the boy came to win despite being under-age. Under the rules it is actually a criminal offence for anyone under the age of sixteen to buy a Lottery ticket or scratch card. Camelot was too late to stop him getting hold of the cash – his mother drew the £10,000 out of a post office on his behalf. The question was whether Camelot would be able to do anything about it. News of this story naturally led to another burst of criticism that the Lottery was luring children into gambling. The shopkeeper who sold the boy the ticket insisted he was innocent, stating that he was convinced the boy was over sixteen because 'he used to deliver papers for us.' Security staff from Camelot interviewed the shopkeeper and cleared him of any impropriety but they warned shopkeepers to be vigilant about under-age buying and to ask for proof of age if they had any doubts.

After buying the ticket the boy returned to claim his prize the following day accompanied by his mother who said the ticket was legitimately hers. She claimed, 'I know that children under sixteen should not buy scratch cards but it was my money – I asked him to buy the ticket.' Nevertheless Camelot have acted responsibly and taken the mother to court to get a declaration over who should have the prize money. Camelot is paying all legal costs so that a court ruling can clarify the law. The company said that if it won the £10,000 would go to the NLDF (National Lottery Distribution Fund).

It was this story, together with the other surveys of under-age buying, that prompted Oflot to order a crackdown on National Lottery retailers in December 1995. Peter Davies, director-general of Oflot, said 'I will not tolerate the sale of National Lottery tickets to under-16s. It is against the law.' He said it not only breached the retailer's contract but flew in the face of the ethos of the Lottery. The move was agreed after research from Plymouth University was presented to him at a meeting with Tim Holley of Camelot which showed that 22% of children aged between twelve and fifteen, in a sample of 1,700 from twelve schools across the country, had spent money on the Lottery or scratch cards in the preceding week. Mr Davis immediately ordered follow-up research to

determine spending patterns to see how far parents are
involved in, and aware of, such purchases. Camelot also
wrote to its 25,000 retailers warning them to seek proof of
age or risk having their terminals removed. Point of sale
material was also to be reviewed to make it clear that under-
16s should not buy tickets and that they were not entitled to
claim any prizes. Camelot also wrote to the director-general
asking what action trading standards officers, the Home
Office and police authorities intend to take. They believed
'robust action' was certainly needed.

CHAPTER 8

EFFECTS ELSEWHERE

Money spent on Lottery tickets has obviously had to come from somewhere. Trends are still emerging about the impact it is having but certain areas have obviously been keenly affected. Key areas are:

Football Pools

It was clear very early on that the pools were going to be a major loser as the Lottery opened. Within weeks Vernons Pools shed ninety-five jobs and cut its donations to charity, citing competition from the Lottery as the cause of its reduction in income. Worse was to follow. In November 1995 Ladbrokes announced another 150 job losses at its Vernons subsidiary reducing the workforce to just 425. In doing so the company stated that they had seen a 25% reduction in revenue year-on-year since the launch of the Lottery. Littlewoods were also hurt by the Lottery. It had to cut 520 jobs – more than 20% of its workforce – after losing 1 in 5 of its 12 million weekly subscribers. Mr Phil Jarrold, managing director of Vernons, said the Lottery enjoyed advantageous tax and trading privileges and he called on the government to reduce pools betting duty from 32.5% to 17.5%. The Lottery is taxed at 12%.

However, in the Chancellor's Budget that month there was a reduction of only 5% to 27.5% with a further 1% agreed conditional to the pools companies passing it on to the football trust, the Foundation for Sport. The size of the cut angered the pools companies. Paul Zetter, chairman of Zetters said, 'Though there have been two cuts this year (1995) in April and December it still leaves the pools companies paying 27.5% against the National Lottery paying 12%. That cannot be considered a level playing field.'

One point in the pools favour however is that the odds of winning are better – even so, not everyone would consider a 1 in 6 million chance of becoming a millionaire attractive!

The Bookmaking Industry
A report by the Henley Centre in the autumn of 1995 showed the savage impact that the National Lottery was having on betting shops. The report claimed that only government intervention could save 2,400 betting shops and 7,400 jobs. They predicted a decline in profitability of 35%.

This has been reflected in what has happened to individual firms. In November shares in Stanley Leisure, which runs betting shops and casinos, fell sharply after a profits warning issued because of the impact of the National Lottery. The company talked about profitability being significantly below the previous year's level. Ladbrokes at the same time indicated that their profits too would be 'somewhat lower' than the previous year's. This led to expectation being reduced from £150 million to £125 million and also led to a significant fall in the share price. Profits of the betting and gaming division actually fell by £40 million. It was the third profit warning they had had to issue in 1995. Mr Peter George, their chief executive, said that scratch cards in particular had had 'a greater impact on our betting business than was anticipated'.

But if anything it is the smaller companies that have suffered more. Don Bruce, who has been involved in bookmaking since 1948, has a chain of shops in London which in 1995 lost £50,000. He felt no-one would want to buy his shops because trade had 'never been worse'. Scratch cards he said had taken away gamblers who were not interested in racing form but just fancied a flutter.

Taking this into account the Levy Board predicted a £24

million reduction in support for the racing industry if the trends continued. Unless substantial relief in the rate of betting duty was given the future 'looks bleak,' said Sir John Sparrow, chairman of the Levy Board. The Chancellor however reduced betting levy by just 1% to 6.7% which was generally felt to be insufficient to pass on to their customers.

Perhaps on the ground of 'if you can't beat 'em, join 'em' William Hill started to accept bets on the winning number in the Irish State Lottery. Punters are able to bet on selecting between one and five of the correct numbers with a maximum payout of £100,000. It has done so partly to arrest the decline in its betting income but also in an attempt to persuade the Government to allow similar wagers on the domestic draw. 'We are 20 million betting slips down this year' their spokesman said. 'The National Lottery is the only thing we are not allowed to bet on by law.' The launch of this new betting 'opportunity' coincided with figures which showed that the Lottery had overtaken the betting shop industry in its contribution to the Exchequer.

Bingo

Even bingo seems to have suffered. John Garrett, head of Rank said, 'Britain's gambling industry is still obliged to operate under the archaic and irrational 1968 Gaming Act's stringent and out-of-date rules, not one of which applies to the National Lottery.' Describing the Lottery as one of the most heavily advertised products ever in the United Kingdom, with £35m being spent by Camelot on advertising each year, he said it was not surprising that the industry was left struggling. 'You cannot even advertise to tell people where they can play bingo,' Mr Garrett complained. Rank's recreational profits fell from £69m to £50m.

Premium Bonds

It is perhaps surprising that sales of Premium Bonds soared in the first year of competition from the Lottery. More bonds were sold in the eighteen months to December 1995 than in the previous ten years put together. Part of the explanation for this is low interest rates elsewhere means that the prize return of 5.2% is attractive. Sales were also boosted by the top prize going up to £1 million. But officials reckoned that the biggest factor was the sharp increase in press and television features about number games.

Meaningful comparisons are difficult to make because capital is not at risk in Premium Bonds. Odds of becoming a millionaire are also lower at 1.54 million to 1 and in addition there are no worries about publicity or losing your ticket so perhaps they attract the more 'timid' gambler.

Public Houses

Takings in public houses have also suffered, it is claimed, as a result of the National Lottery and that is why, with the encouragement of various brewery companies, a trial was set up installing Lottery machines in seventy pubs for six months. If successful, the machines could be installed in other pubs by mid-1996. Concern has been expressed that mixing gambling with alcohol could create problems and that people might get carried away, particularly when it comes to scratch cards. Another aspect of this potential development saw fruit machine operators voice similar fears to those made by pools operators – their takings were already down by 11% year on year before this move. To off-set this the Government announced that all-cash prizes of up to £10 would be allowed (against £4 in cash or £8 in tokens as before). They were also allowed into betting shops. Mr Timothy Kirhope, Home Office Minister, said 'These pro-posals are good news for the punters.' Playing fruit machines is already the most popular form of gambling after the National Lottery.

Television

The first live programme of the Lottery draw attracted more than 20 million people before settling down to the 14 million figure. Figures however declined further to 11.5 million by late 1995. This may be due partly to the novelty of watching balls come out of a machine wearing off or because ITV have countered the attraction well by flashing the winning num-bers across the screen as soon as they are drawn or by broad-casting a news flash in a commercial break. (Results are also broadcast live on Radio 1.) Despite the fall however there has been little concern at either Camelot or the BBC which pointed out that the programme still attracts over 55% of the watching television audience. The BBC is also considering a mid-week game show using scratch card winners as contes-tants and would also probably screen any mid-week draws that Camelot might make.

The Press

The National Lottery seems to have been a godsend for the press because it is still hard to buy a daily paper without find-ing some reference to it. Many of the tabloids in particular have been quick to put in criticism especially when commenting on where Lottery money was being allocated. Thus the *Sunday Express* article about the Charities Board distribution stated 'Drug addicts, refugees, single mothers, alcoholics and ethnic groups are to get National Lottery grants totalling hundreds of thousands of pounds.' In reality it was of course the *charities* that look after these groups of people and in any case they represented a small percentage of the total outlay. In another emotional piece the *Mail on Sunday* criticised handouts to the rich (i.e. the opera) and obscure politically correct groups when 'the charities that work their hearts out for ordinary people' were depicted as losers. Clearly this is a story that will run and run.

Shops

There are now approaching 30,000 outlets where Lottery tickets can be purchased and about half of these are small independently owned shops. Camelot estimates that the average weekly lottery sale is £4,000. Of that the retailer will receive 5% – or £200 – plus 1% commission on prizes above £10 and below £200. Ramish Patel of St Leonards, Sussex says the Lottery has given a new lease of life to his business. 'The Lottery has helped business a lot,' he said. 'We now stay open 'till 7.30pm on a Saturday evening and there is a great atmosphere. Sales of sweets, cigarettes and newspapers have also gone up and when people come to collect their winnings on Sunday they often end up spending them on scratch cards.'

Large retailing chains, such as W H Smith, are reluctant to disclose the impact of the National Lottery on their businesses as they are afraid of giving out information to their competitors but T & S, the northern convenience store group, reckon that sales of Lottery and scratch cards in total will be around £100 million per annum, bringing in £750,000 commission in total. There is also the add on benefit of impulse spending on sweets, etc. as people queue to buy the tickets.

The Economy

The National Lottery seems to be responsible for both good and bad news for the UK economy! Proceeds from the Lottery brought in about £700 million in the first year thus improving the borrowing total and giving the Chancellor more room to cut taxes. In addition Camelot pays out 28% of the Lottery revenues to the distribution fund which is counted as part of central government revenue. Eventually all this is distributed to good causes but in the meantime the Treasury has use of significant sums of money.

Against that the Lloyds Bank Economic Bulletin in October 1995 blamed the Lottery for cuts in retail spending of 2%. Their chief economist, Patrick Foley, argued that the effects of the Lottery could explain why retail sales had been flat despite increased spending by consumers. This was confirmed by Baird's Menswear which blamed the Lottery for job cuts in the clothing industry which left 290 people redundant in Hartlepool. They argued that disposable income was coming out of the economy and that no new money had been created since the Lottery arrived.

An economist at J P Morgan also argued that the Lottery accounted for a third of the fall in growth. 'Billions have been taken out of the economy and put into the bank.' He estimated that most of the £1.6 billion prize money had been banked rather than spent.

The Lottery also cut into related categories of consumer spending. For example, in the first half of 1995 money spent on leisure activities such as visits to the cinema or leisure centres fell by 7.5%, while sales of sweets fell by 2% and soft drinks by 0.7%. Even the Treasury admitted that because the Lottery had been so much bigger than expected it must have reduced the economy's growth although they felt it impossible to quantify by how much. The stampede for scratch cards undoubtedly drove up consumer spending and actually accounted for 25% of the growth of 0.8% in the second quarter of 1995. Total spending on the Lottery in 1995 was equivalent to more than 65% of total gaming and gambling expenditure in 1994. Total Lottery sales are around £5 billion but half are returned as prize money. The net figure of £2.6 billion is still dwarfed by the £66 billion spent on housing or the £50 billion on cars but it represents:

- half of what was spent on gas bills
- a quarter of the amount spent on cigarettes
- a fifth of the amount spent on ladies' clothes

It is also more than is spent on vehicle excise duty, rail travel, beauty products, hairdressing and bread.

The Henley Centre predicted in December 1995 that the Lottery would, in its second year, draw £655 million away from spending on entertainment and £456 million away from food, confectionery and cigarettes. They also anticipate a net increase in personal savings of £472 million as prize money is deposited, mostly in building societies.

In the first year the report estimated that of the £2.2 billion in prizes, £1.2 billion went into consumer spending, £300 million into long-term savings and £300 million into housing. Of the £2.6 billion that came out of the consumer spending £400 million came from food, newsagents and off-licences, £500 million from other betting and gambling, £600 million from other entertainment such as cinema and sport and £35 million from charities. The balance of £900 million came from all other spending sectors. Clearly the National Lottery is having a dramatic impact on the way the nation spends its money.

CHAPTER 9

SCRATCH CARDS – AN INSTANT PROBLEM?

Many of the problems of the Instant scratch cards have already been referred to at various stages throughout the book, and the view that they represent a harder form of gambling, and the temptation they provide for teenagers, have already been examined. Nonetheless, because of their very nature they need to be looked at separately.

In March 1995 Camelot expected 'Instants' to generate about £1 billion a year, or 25% of Lottery revenue. They claimed that scratch cards would be the launch of the largest-ever impulse brand in the UK. 'It will be three times larger than the sale of Coca Cola, ten times larger than the sale of Mars Bars and larger than the entire cereals market.'

I fear that this could well be a boast that comes back to haunt them. Dr Mark Griffiths wrote to *The Independent* in April 1995. 'As someone who has been carrying out research into gambling behaviour for over seven years, one thing which I know to be well established is that gambling activities in which the time between money being gambled and knowing the result of the gamble is short (like fruit machines and roulette) tend to be more addictive than those gambling activities with long time gaps (like the weekly National Lottery or the football pools). Camelot's 'Instants' scratch card lottery is *not* an extension of the National Lottery but a totally separate form of gambling which gives all purchasers the chance to gamble repeatedly (rather than once a week) for a £50,000 prize. The scratch cards are little more than paper fruit machines and thus will be potentially addictive to some. Moreover they are available to young people and provide adolescents with another form of legalised gambling.'

Sadly this already seems to be reflected. A general store in Hoxton takes £6,000 a week in Lottery purchases – more than half being for Instants. The shopkeeper, Kistor Patel, said 'Every week more play. On average most of my customers spend between £2 and £3. Very few spend just £1. A lot of them are pensioners and you feel they are spending money they cannot afford.'

However, there does seem to have been a decline in sales from a peak of around £44 million a week to around £20 million. Camelot argued a drop in sales of this magnitude after three or four months of their introduction had been a common experience for other lotteries around the world but nevertheless they were watching the situation carefully. A similar situation had occurred in France but sales subsequently recovered and now stand at £1.9 billion a year for scratch cards alone.

The criticisms of Instant cards are primarily two-fold. One, as has been said, is that they are addictive – the shorter the time lapse between cause and effect the stronger the psychological link. Another problem is the near-miss syndrome. When you almost win a big prize you are very tempted to have another go. This is a well-known technique, known as a 'heart-stopper'. Every loss is thus perceived as 'almost a win' which reinforces the urge to try yet again. This is why scratch cards have come in for even harsher criticism than the Lottery – with some actually coming from a group of MPs protesting about Camelot's decision to have the tickets printed abroad. But the more realistic protests have come from:

- **The Labour Party** – Chris Smith, Labour's Heritage spokesman, said a written health warning, similar to those found on cigarette packets, should be printed on the back of all Instant cards to counter their addictive effect. In a letter to Virginia Bottomley he stressed the need to help players who were getting into financial difficulty. He said, 'All the experts agree that the most addictive pastimes are those in which the interval between staking a bet and hearing the result is shortest. With scratch cards this interval can be as little as ten seconds.' A spokeswoman for Camelot said they had no plans to introduce warnings as they didn't believe there was a widespread problem with people spending more than they could afford.

- **The Liberal Democrats** – they went even further and decided at their National Conference to ban scratch cards altogether and place a cap on the National Lottery, despite warnings from some delegates that the party would be seen as illiberal killjoys. The motion was moved by Andrew Stunell who told the Conference of a newsagent taking £15,000 a week on the Lottery just from a suburban council estate in his constituency. He criticised the growth in scratch cards saying some people lose up to £20 in one go.

- **Oflot** – the Lottery regulator commissioned detailed research into spending habits and gambling addiction. A spokesman said they had a duty not to licence any game that would contribute to excessive gambling. The findings of this research have been called 'unreliable'. They have somewhat surprisingly ruled that buying a scratch card is primarily a charitable donation.

- **The Joseph Rowntree Foundation** – a report by them highlighted the addictive nature of scratch cards and claimed that 20% of calls to Gamblers Anonymous related to them.

- **The Church of Ireland** – their Board of Social Responsibility said the percentage of people involved in gambling had increased considerably since scratch cards were introduced. 'Much of the money that is needed by families is wasted on them,' a spokesman said.

- **The Methodist Church** – the annual conference of the Methodist Church called for the scrapping of scratch cards and also recommended that charities working for the poor should be able to claim Lottery funds in exceptional circumstances. There was a particular concern that many more women were becoming addicted to scratch cards and gambling as they regularly went about their shopping.

- **Gamblers Anonymous** – have reported a significant increase in calls since scratch cards were introduced, including a call from someone who got into debt after buying 120 cards and another who was currently spending £500 a week on them.

- **Trans-Release** – this counselling group for gambling addicts said that the easy availability of the cards enables compulsive buyers to hide their addiction. 'It's not a casino where everyone can see what you are doing,' said one counsellor.

- **The UK Forum on Young People and Gambling** – they fear that many young people will become addicted, as they are particularly susceptible to Saatchi and Saatchi's high profile advertising campaign, 'Forget it all for an Instant.'

The success of the Instants has led others to try and join the bandwagon. Amongst these have been Littlewoods who offered a game with a top prize of £50,000 and UKCL whose deal with the National Lottery has led to a four-fold increase in sales of its Lukcy Lotto game. The demand is certainly there but is it really doing any harm? Well, it still leads to greed, as the case of the thirty-four year old Nottingham lady showed when her boyfriend claimed half her winnings.

Other cases clearly indicate how easy it is to get hooked on scratch cards. For example:

- A fifty year old lady who, despite working for a bookmaker for twenty years, spends £20 a week on scratch cards and funds her compulsion by cutting down on food for her family and housekeeping. She said 'I always think it will be the lucky one. It makes my life a misery. The only way I will stop being addicted is to stop playing completely. In many ways I wish I'd never started.'

• A twenty-three year old single mum with three children is addicted. She said 'I'm on Income Support and I get £69 a week plus £27 child benefit, that makes £96 a week. I have to go without clothes for the children and me. I get my money on Monday and by Wednesday or Thursday it's gone. I've got behind on the gas... Most people around here are in the same situation. It's not a nice place to bring up your kids; there are joyriders and drugs and the kids' language is terrible. Scratch cards are the only way out... I feel guilty when I buy scratch cards. I should be saving the money but you just can't help yourself. I do it because I think if I won the big one all my troubles would be over... I'm not clever, I only read and write a bit. I get depressed a lot. I don't get out much – where can you go with the kids?'

• At one newsagent in a run down suburb of York there is a trail of discarded used Instants as a testimony of the spent hopes of many players. One woman in her early thirties placed her two children with sweets as she stood on the pavement scribbling furiously at ten cards. One produced a small win which she immediately spent on more cards. The newsagent says, 'They're infectious. I see people buy five or six a day, win a tenner and then continue to play until they lose everything. They are often women from the estate and I know they don't have a lot of spare cash. It's not my place to say anything. If I think it's getting out of hand I'll have a joke with them and gently point out how much they're losing.' He continued, 'Unless they win a large amount they almost always put the money into more cards. Something stops people just walking away with any winnings.' Research has indicated that 20% of scratch card gamblers buy 65% of the tickets. One lady said she bought five tickets a week adding that she would never have the nerve to go to a bookies. Her friend admitted that she didn't tell her husband just how much she spent on the cards. In a revealing comment she said, 'Everybody needs a bit of secret excitement and this is mine. It's better than having an affair but more expensive.'

Contrast this with Mrs Bottomley who has described Instants as 'harmless'!

Perhaps I could finish this chapter by reproducing a letter sent by an anonymous writer to the *Guardian* in October 1995. 'Each time I present my benefits cheque at the local Post Office I run the gauntlet of tempting adverts for the National Lottery. And believe me it is a temptation when collecting £45 Income Support. I just can't resist £1 a week on a Saturday draw – well there's no harm in it is there? Those bloody scratch cards are, however, another matter entirely. By offering the chance of an instant win of up to £50,000 they are all but irresistible to us financially challenged. Every time I've won £1 or £2 I reinvest until it's all gone. I've a feeling I'm not the only one. Well, it's not really gambling is it? Not those pretty little cards winking at you from beyond a tube of Smarties or a book of second-class stamps. So I'll have to survive on baked beans until my next benefit cheque; but I'll still produce less hot air than a barrel-load of Bottomleys.'

CHAPTER 10

WHAT DOES THE LOTTERY SAY ABOUT OUR SOCIETY?

There are very mixed views on the National Lottery. At first, apart from a few 'killjoy' churchmen and moralists, very few saw much, if any, harm in it. Nowadays barely a day goes past without some article praising or criticising aspects of the National Lottery. The initial critics, many opposed to gambling *per se*, have been joined by others concerned at the regulator's role, the latest winner's reaction or, more generally, the fear of growing addiction. Everyone now appears to have an opinion.

I think it might be helpful at this point to list some of the benefits the National Lottery has brought.

- **The beneficial impact of giving to charities, arts, etc.** It is important to recognise that while some charities have suffered as a result of the National Lottery many others have received funding that they would otherwise have struggled to obtain. My own personal view is that much of the criticism has been 'self' motivated – either 'it's not fair we are suffering' or 'you're not picking the right charities, i.e. the ones that I like.'

- **The planning required by charities before applying for funds.** I believe that the NLCB is quite stringent in reviewing applications to it and consequently all requests for funding have to be very carefully worked out. This professional approach, I believe, will actually help a considerable number of charities accurately define their priorities and ambitions and, ultimately, their ability to achieve them. Lucy Pratt of the Scottish Council for Voluntary Organisations agreed. 'It's put a rocket up behind some charities who have been quite complacent in the past about always being able to raise money.'

- **The bonding of syndicates.** Many family groups, or syndicates at work have got together to buy Lottery tickets. This undoubtedly increases camaraderie and can boost a feeling of team spirit. Incidentally, the danger of a syndicate winning the jackpot and deciding *en bloc* to leave work is now so strong that businesses can buy insurance to protect them should that happen! 10% of players are known to play the on-line game in a group. Others have office sweepstakes on the number of the bonus ball with fifty tickets being sold and the winner scooping the pool. Smaller office syndicates even gamble on which star sign Mystic Meg will mention first!

- **Fun, anticipation and dreams.** I am sure that the reason most people enjoy doing the Lottery is because it gives them a chance to dream. It is a dream of release from reality – a dream of sunshine, sand, leisure and the ability to give two fingers to the boss, the mortgage, the debts and the desperate attempts to 'keep up with the Jones' – in your dream they have no chance of catching up with you! But you can also dream of being able to do good things for your family and friends so that people can see your true nature. For many too it is 'harmless fun'. Just £1 or so a week and a quietly hopeful wait for Saturday night.

But one has to ask, just because people are unharmed by it does that make it right? What message does it give to society? The slave trade didn't directly harm or affect most people in Britain at the time but it said something about that society and it certainly didn't make it right. The Lottery is popular, but then so were public hangings. On reflection, I do believe the balance needed between 'my' and 'society's' rights and

responsibilities has moved much too far into the 'right's' position. At the moment we all tend to fight our corner, to justify our position, and find it almost impossible to say sorry and take the blame ourselves. It is my 'right'. The 'responsibility' is always somebody else's.

This Government and the media have given the National Lottery unprecedented support and publicity. So on one level it is a shared national experience, a bit of fun for millions, but its long-term implications and what it says about our society is frightening. We are in a pervasive gambling environment in which up to 86% of adults will gamble. Our experience of the Lottery has mirrored that in New Jersey where 'the results exceeded all but the most wildly optimistic predictions and demonstrated what a well-designed and aggressively mer-chandised Lottery could produce.' So it is that a 'get rich quick' attitude has entered all aspects of our everyday life and it is likely to spread and spread with incalculable effects. In the nineties we have felt totally insecure, stressed out and uncomfortable and thus we are desperate for escape. So if our desires are to be frustrated by society perhaps Mystic Meg will come and lift us out of our sad existence.

Gambling pressures

Gambling in Britain has been growing even excluding the National Lottery. In the period 1990-95 the number of fruit machines has increased by over 50,000 to 2,570,000. Their £3 maximum payout was increased to £10 fairly recently. Even before this was done the average profit per machine was £14 per week.

Until the National Lottery the Government had always controlled the promotion of opportunities to gamble, although there has been a gradual relaxation of the rules. The Home Office has been responsible for gambling policy and therefore social factors rather than revenue implications have been the main consideration. The National Lottery makes a significant reversal of that policy. Furthermore the Heritage Secretary claimed when the Bill to introduce the

National Lottery was announced that it would not attract the gamblers. 'We expect it to attract new sections of the population, people who are willing to have a flutter knowing that – win or lose – money will be going to good causes.' The Council on Gambling immediately described this view as naive and this has turned out to be correct.

For the Lottery to succeed it had to be promoted and the Government has set about doing this most effectively. Control was switched to the Department of National Heritage with a duty to maximise revenue rather than consider social implications. And gaining money has proved to be the major, if not the sole reason, for many people buying Lottery tickets. The reason people participate is in the hope of winning – the percentage that goes to good causes is, I believe, more of a sop to the conscience of the Government and the organisers. The number of people who play using a form of elaborate 'lucky numbers' system is indicative of gambling.

It is quite clear too that Instants, with their 'heart-stoppers' and encouragement to buy more, clearly encourage the potential gambler to try once more.

The rollover jackpot is yet another incentive to participate. Experience already shows a strong correlation between jackpot size and participation. Indeed the question of how much the maximum prize can be is perhaps the most crucial factor in the whole thing. When the top prize is not won it is rolled over to the next week's draw. This can continue up to a maximum period of three weeks. Indications from Canada show potential problems here. In 1984 the jackpot was not won for several weeks, resulting in a very high potential sum available to the winner. During that particular week outlets reported double or triple the usual sales with reports of some people queuing for up to five hours to buy tickets. Many people apparently spent the equivalent of £50 a time. The double roll-over in early 1996 resulted in a sharp drop in charitable giving in that period. This surely flies in the face of those who believe that the Lottery will not attract gamblers and in any case they will only invest what they can afford to lose.

The frequency of advertising, television, radio and press comment also gives cause for concern. Much money is available and all publicity is generally good publicity. In reality a lottery is an extremely bad bet yet people continue to participate in the hope of winning in the face of very long odds. Even the information about the odds of winning may not prove an adequate safeguard as participants consistently seem to underestimate the importance of those long odds and focus instead on the advertising telling them that 'it could be you'. This irrational behaviour may be self-justified in the [false] belief that their lucky numbers or system significantly reduces the odds. It may of course be the one and only desperate attempt to escape. While not wanting to deny that I wonder what will happen over a period of time when many realise that these hopes actually promoted by the Government and Camelot proved to be false. Adverts present an image of success and happiness for the lucky winners thereby implying that people are fools if they do not participate. In fact, for the vast majority of people the best thing to do is to hold on to the money. Any suggestion that a spare, or even not-so-spare, pound should really buy a Lottery ticket is grossly misleading.

Problem gambling

In the run-up to the Lottery even the Government implied that problems may well occur for some. 'For *most* people participation in the Lottery will provide a harmless form of entertainment. *Many* countries which have had a National Lottery for many years do not report any *major* adverse social effects.' However evidence from the United States over the last thirty years does indicate firstly a new type of problem gambler, the lottery addict. It also seems that the increased availability of this form of gambling has led to addictions to other forms. In one major survey researchers found that the amount of money spent on lotteries was a predictor of both loss of control (behavioural aspects such as hidden gambling, inability to resist the temptation, spending more than intended and a return to gambling after trying to give it up) and of problem gambling (losing time from work or school, borrowing money, illegal behaviour). Various characteristics such as impatience and impulsiveness were also seen to be predictors of such behaviour.

Studies confirm that gambling addiction leads to increased crime. A study by the University of Illinois concluded that were gambling to be brought to Chicago the criminal justice bill would soar by more than $1 billion.

Dr Valerie Lorenz, director of the National Center for Pathological Gambling in Baltimore, has no doubt about the contribution of large scale lotteries to problem gambling. 'Ten years ago a female compulsive gambler was a rarity in treatment. Lottery addicts were virtually unheard of. Teenage compulsive gamblers were non-existent and compulsive gamblers amongst senior citizens were also a rarity a mere decade ago. Yet today all these compulsive gamblers abound in every state, at every Gamblers Anonymous meeting, at professional treatment programmes and in the criminal justice system.' Dr Lorenz added that despite claims that lotteries are 'soft', addicts report the same feeling of excitement in placing bets and the same depression and despair after losing. This is invariably followed by a period of recovery when the desire to chase losses by improving their 'system' for picking numbers takes place. This can be followed by a decline in productivity, debt and even theft and suicide attempts. During the Center's first full year of operation (1988-9) 7% of compulsive gamblers stated that lotteries were their main form of gambling. By 1990 this figure had risen to 22% and has continued to rise slowly since then.

Iain Brown, lecturer in psychology at the University of Glasgow and a specialist in compulsive gambling, said, 'We've seen what happens in other parts of the world. It can have the effect of unhinging people's grip on reality. It creates a false dream state and paralyses action because people expect manna from heaven. The people who are most susceptible are those leading drab and depressing lives. It becomes a substitute for hope. I'd call it a tax on poverty and despair.' See how this is already echoed in the quote of the newsagent who sold tickets to the man who killed himself because he thought he had missed the jackpot – 'People become obsessed by the National Lottery. For some of my customers it is all they seem to live for. They spend their last pennies on it each week.'

An intelligent and thought-provoking leader article in *The Independent* in April 1995 offered the following perspective:

Once we sought salvation in religion. Now ten million prayers are raised for a National Lottery jackpot...In an inner city corner shop impoverished pensioners and despairing dads queue to put money they cannot afford into a competition that statistically they cannot win. Like Jack in the story they hand their livelihood over for a handful of beans – except there will be no beanstalk. Constant fantasising about how vast sums of unearned dosh would transform their lives corrodes the ability to live in the present. And many are becoming gamblers for the first time. Unlike betting on the horse or hound or filling in the pools, expertise confers no advantage in the Lottery – all clearly stand an equal chance. As a result many who never enter a betting shop or return a slip to Littlewoods are being drawn into gambling – and gambling addiction. Democracy allows people to make their own decisions about the balance of advantage. In an incredibly short period of time the Lottery has become a national institution that cannot be uninvented. Nevertheless here is a prediction. In fifteen years or so the Chief Medical Officer will issue a report detailing the damage done by excessive gambling on the Lottery. This report will make one or all of the following recommendations – that all tickets carry a health warning, that all advertising makes it clear just how preposterous the odds are, and that the National Lottery itself should fund a national health education campaign by Gamblers Anonymous. Perhaps we shouldn't wait.

Another problem is that of a lottery maturing. As it does so the increase in revenue slows down. This creates considerable pressure for profit – and operators seek to increase participation rates. Whereas in the case of our Lottery the participation rates are already high, others can tend to lead to advertising strategies aimed at converting casual users into regular ones. New games and new technologies such as telephone betting and video lotteries for use in arcades can also be used to maintain revenue growth. Such pressures can only increase the potential for addictive gambling. Current safeguards go nowhere near far enough to prevent this happening.

A fifty-year-old reformed gambler knew better than most that he needed help when he spent £120 on the National Lottery in one week. The temptation had proved too great and so he turned to Gamblers Anonymous. 'Buying the Lottery Instants was like standing at the edge of a whirlpool,' he said. 'I started with bets of no more than £1 at a time but it began to accelerate and I felt I was being sucked in.' His decline began with the first big jackpot of £17 million. 'When there was a roll-over I started to spend more than I could afford. When the Instants came out it was so easy to walk into a shop and buy them with my newspaper.' Soon he found himself feeling that same old unwanted thrill.

A similar story came from a clerical worker in Edinburgh who had been a compulsive gambler twenty years ago but restarted with the Lottery. Research by the Henley Centre that has studied lotteries in Britain, Canada and Ireland found a core of such committed players in each country. They tend to come from lower income backgrounds. Typical is a jobless young lady from Glasgow who borrows up to £60 to buy Instants every week. 'I don't want to buy them but I can't help it,' she said, 'but the tickets are a possible route out of here.' For many too the urge to spend on the Lottery retains its allure long after the dream of winning has turned sour. A thirty-year-old man has spent his entire winnings of £48,000 in four months on a car, holiday and improvements to his flat. He is now forced to try and find a new job after giving up his position as a security guard in the euphoria of his win. He continues to spend £15 on tickets every week.

The Samaritans too, have begun to receive calls at the peak times of Saturday night and Sunday morning from people whose depression has been deepened by picking the wrong numbers. Even the Gaming Board has called for research into possible links between compulsive gambling and the National Lottery. Lady Littler, their chairwoman, said that there were tremendous temptations to go on and on buying scratch cards. 'If you have a small win you are tempted to blow it on more cards and if you do not you are tempted to go on and have another.'

Debt

An investigation by *The Sunday Express* found that the dream of easy money is so powerful that buying Lottery tickets has in some cases taken over from day to day expenses on essentials. It found there was evidence of mounting rent arrears and mortgage debt because people are spending more than they can afford on the Lottery and Instants. Housing officers in Taunton reported this as a key factor in rent arrears that were 10% higher than a year ago. A council spokesman said that people with the least means are the ones to whom the dream of a Lottery win is most important. 'Paying the rent is boring and winning the Lottery means the end to all financial troubles. So it's no contest. But it can only be played at the expense of other things.' Top city mortgage analyst, Rob Thomas, also said that the Lottery was to blame for an increase in short-term mortgage arrears.

Values

Every Bill introduced into Parliament, and especially if it becomes law, says something about the values of our society. What sort of message then is our Government sending out by promoting a lottery? Economists C Clotfelter and P Cook in their book *Selling Hope* are quite clear.

There is more to selling lottery tickets than persuading the public that playing is a good investment. At a more basic level the sales job may be viewed as an education in values, teaching that gambling is a benign or even virtuous activity that offers an escape from the dreariness of work and limited means. Not only does lottery advertising endorse gambling *per se* but it also endorses the dream of easy wealth that motivates gambling. The ads are unabashedly materialistic and their message is a slightly subversive one – that success is just a matter of picking the right numbers. The gospel of wealth based on sweat and a little bit of luck is replaced by one based on luck alone. Needless to say waiting for fortune to smile is not the formula for success that is usually taught!

What on earth does this message convey to our children? But it affects adults too and it affects them now. Recently we had a call on the Credit Action helpline from a man addicted to the Lottery. He was a low-paid manual worker. He didn't like his job and he didn't like where he lived and he had negative equity on his property. 'My life is so mundane,' he complained. 'I am nine weeks in arrears with my mortgage so I might as well be ten weeks behind and use the money for Lottery tickets again. At least if I win I will be out of here and never have to pay the xxxxx mortgage again.'

I can see that for some sources of hope are hard to find. But policies offering real hope need to be found rather than a lottery which offers initial false dreams and eventual further disillusionment to the millions who are struggling in our country. The Lottery will not make the country any richer *per se*. It is currently a more popular way than taxation of redistributing wealth. A nation that relies on hard work is usually prosperous. A government that switches priorities to luck should be really concerned that it is undermining a valuable plank of the nation's very being.

Greed

Another question that needs answering is that when something depends on greed to be successful, can you regard it as morally acceptable? I think you can dismiss the 'good causes' argument because if you want to give you can do so easily and select your own preferences as well. It is also clear that when there is a rollover jackpot ticket sales increase significantly, thus increasing the likelihood of gambling addiction. I do not see how this can be morally justifiable because it must mean that the pressures are such, particularly for the desperate, that they will certainly overcommit themselves. It is clearly a sad sign also when the 132 millionaires that the Lottery has created so far say that their biggest regrets are that they didn't win sooner and that they didn't win more.

Public opinion

A very large percentage of the population approved of the
National Lottery when it started and there are still many
who cling to that view. But with all the criticism that has been
levelled at it there are signs of opinion turning and this was
in fact pointed out in a *Daily Mail* leader in December 1995.
Marjorie Proops who was on the 1978 Royal Commission
that looked into the National Lottery is one who has
changed her mind. She said, 'Will you forgive us. We were
naive and very foolish. If I had my time again my answer
would be no.'

Camelot themselves have shown nervousness in the past
that public opinion might turn against the Lottery. They lob-
bied delegates ahead of a critical debate at the Liberal
Democrats Conference and they also launched an advertising onslaught at the time of its first anniversary in which it
emphasised the benefits that it brings to 'good causes'. They
employ a team of ten to deal with factual enquiries about the
Lottery as well as an external PR company and a public
affairs team that handles the more awkward questions. They
have admitted that the 'It could be you' advert was specially
chosen because it veiled the 1 in 14 million chance of winning
the Lottery in simple optimism. Mr Rigg said, 'What the
public responded to was the idea that they could win and the
odds were not against them. Every time we considered the
campaign we tested it against the words 'simple, easy and
fun'.

The Heritage Secretary, Virginia Bottomley, has remained
an avid supporter of the National Lottery, despite privately
despairing at some of the adverse criticism that some of the
grants have attracted. She has referred to it as 'truly the
Dream Machine' and is effusive about the awards to charities. She said 'Labour's line on the Lottery is simple – snuff
out success, punish profit and cheat the good causes of the
deal they deserve.' Her opposition counterpart demanded
that more should go to good causes and that the Lottery
should be run on non-profit lines. As the next election

approaches it will be interesting to see whether this actively becomes a vote-catching debate. Sadly, I fear that most people are primarily concerned about money that might be coming to them rather than what is going to Camelot, the Government or good causes.

CHAPTER 11

THE POSITION OF THE CHRISTIAN DENOMINATIONS AND CHARITIES

E ven though the churches have joined together under the Rt Rev David Sheppard, Anglican Bishop of Liverpool, the position of different groups varies and perhaps this accounts for the fact that the Christian message is somewhat diluted even to people who attend church every week. Some of the stances currently taken are listed below:

The Salvation Army
In a succinct statement that clearly shows where the Salvation Army stands and what they believe they say:

1. That no Salvationist is to participate in the National Lottery.
2. That the Salvation Army has given an undertaking not to apply for Lottery funds for charitable work.

The United Reformed Church
In July 1995 their General Assembly passed a motion which read 'Assembly urges the Members and Councils of the church to disassociate themselves from the Lottery by refusing to buy tickets and by declining to apply for Lottery-gen-

erated funds for church purposes.' The vote in favour was stronger in the first part (refusing to buy tickets) than for the second (declining to apply for funds) because some local churches are inevitably in association with local consortia in the voluntary sector who are applying for Lottery-generated funds for community projects.

The Baptist Church
The Baptist Union Council feared that the National Lottery would be a temptation to Government and society to avoid responsibility to the community by relying on greed to gain money for social welfare.

The Church of England
The House of Bishops has criticised the National Lottery as 'a form of nationally-sponsored gambling designed to encourage false hope and overindulgence. We remain concerned that the advertising of the Lottery is calculated to encourage greed.'

The Methodist Church
They stated that the Instant cards would be particularly potentially dangerous for the poor and unemployed with time to kill. Adding that the purchase of a Lottery ticket is not in itself evil, they have said that it is wrong to stimulate expenditure on gambling through the National Lottery in the knowledge that poor people will be harmed. The President of the Methodist Conference, Rev Dr Leslie Griffiths said, 'I will not be buying any Lottery tickets whatsoever and it is my hope that all Methodists will follow suit. I am no killjoy – I believe in life and fun and I even believe in the odd mild and little 'flutter' – but I do not believe in a government resorting to a National Lottery as a disguise for what ought to be properly thought out policies. Charitable work and social work are going to suffer. For all these reasons and many more the Lottery is a hugely regrettable step.'

The Church of Scotland

The National Lottery is an 'ethically undesirable method of raising public funds and is damaging to the nation's public ethos' according to the Church of Scotland report which calls the Lottery a 'national legitimisation of greed' and warns that 'funds from it should not be regarded as a substitute for a responsible level of public funding.'

The Catholic Church

The Roman Catholic church has always seemed to take a more relaxed view on gambling and this is reflected in their statement that they have 'decided to wait until the Lottery is within two years of its five year review before making any declared statement about ethical issues and the impact of the Lottery on the citizens of the United Kingdom.'

Elim Pentecostal Church

'Elim has always taken the stance that it is against all kinds of gambling and this would include the Lottery.'

The Quakers

'The existence of a National Lottery sanctioned by the Government may well encourage people to seek a return on their charitable giving essentially taking the charity out of charitable giving... The hidden long-term effects on society will be to encourage selfishness, the belief that anyone who does something for nothing is a fool.'

A united front

Despite the differing priorities, however, there was sufficient unity among church leaders for them to come together at the time of the Lottery's first anniversary to condemn many aspects of it. Describing it as 'undermining the public culture' they called for radical changes which included an end to scratch cards, a maximum jackpot of £1 million and a minimum playing age of eighteen.

The Rt Rev David Sheppard led senior officials from

many churches in calling for the changes but admitted that they faced 'ethical dilemmas' in applying for Lottery funding themselves. Churches around the country have already received well over £1 million of Lottery funding with many millions of pounds of applications still outstanding. Bishop Sheppard pointed out that the Church of England only applied for Lottery funds to ensure its buildings were maintained properly from the Heritage Fund which has now been included in the Lottery remit. He added that it would not be applying for funding for pastoral work. Nicholas Coute, the Roman Catholic representative, 'did not see obstacles to particular churches and dioceses to make applications... We are not going to cut off our nose to spite our face,' he said.

The Council of Churches for Britain and Ireland's statement said that their clear perception is that many vulnerable and desperate people are being induced to spend money on the Lottery that they cannot afford. It added that the huge advertising budget had created a considerable likelihood of gambling harm, with little prospect of public benefit. The Lottery was also 'undermining the public culture in which money from taxation, charities working at national and local level, central and local government have co-operated to sustain the common good.'

Christian charities

Many Christian charities have taken a robust stand and have refused to apply to the Lottery for funding. This is despite evidence that giving has declined to these charities, particularly those who use street collections as part of their fundraising activities. This obviously means that the charities have to rely on increased giving from their supporters or else they will have to cut back. Thus **Methodist Homes** have decided not to apply for funds. A spokesman said, 'I am putting my faith in the Methodist people. We believe that the care of elderly people is not a matter of chance.' **NCH Action for Children** has also decided not to apply. Other comments have included:

Tear Fund. They will not be seeking funds from the Lottery but, while not wishing to encourage their supporters to participate in it, they would accept gifts that were the result of a Lottery win.

Evangelical Alliance Scotland. Not only would they not apply, but they would not be happy knowingly to accept a gift as part of the proceeds of the National Lottery.

Oasis Trust. Rev Steve Chalke said that Oasis 'could make a good case for doing something constructive with the money but we are unambiguous in opposition to the Lottery. The Lottery runs directly against the spirit of charity. All it is doing is making greed socially acceptable. It will appeal the most to people who can least afford the ticket price, encouraging them to look for a way out of their troubles through gambling. The odds against winning are so slim that most people will simply waste what they cannot afford to lose.'

The Girls' Brigade. A statement issued by the Girls' Brigade said, 'We exist to offer girls a Christian viewpoint on life and it would be completely inconsistent to teach them to value and serve other people while the organisation itself accepted funding from a source where people can only gain by the loss of others.'

John Grooms. They have said that 'whilst it could make an extremely strong case for the use of money from the Lottery it will not be applying itself nor has it any desire to encourage participation in the Lottery which it believes undermines the Christian principle of giving motivated by gratitude to God.'

The National Conference of the Movement for Christian Democracy has voted for the abolition of the National Lottery by a large majority, after a debate in which many reform proposals were considered. MP David Alton, a co-founder of the movement, said 'the last Lottery collapsed in corruption and so will this one.' Echoing the pressures felt by many Christian workers who were told they had to work on

Sundays, the debate heard of a sub-postmaster who was threatened with the sack because he refused to sell lottery tickets. A teacher also spoke in the debate about the impact it was even having on primary school children who are being encouraged to believe that success is a matter of luck. Those

present took encouragement from Wilberforce's successful stand against a previous National Lottery.

Some churches, however, remain divided on whether to apply for funds. A debate in the Cambridge Anglican Deanery Synod was stopped before a vote could be taken. The reason given for this was that if the motion not to receive any benefits from the proceeds of the National Lottery had been passed 'it might have sent signals that we were nanny-ing people. If we'd rejected it, it would have said that the Church of England approved of the National Lottery which would have been an equally unfortunate signal.' But division remains. In one week in October 1995 the Ely Diocesan

Board of Social Responsibility attacked the Lottery for encouraging gambling among the young and diverting cash from other charities. The Bishop of Ely said that the Lottery 'creates a lot of misery and despair and on reflection I would like to see it banned. People feel that they have to play otherwise they are missing out on the greatest thing in life.' Adding that this is not a Christian priority he said, 'People end up thinking about the Lottery all week and don't concentrate on the good things in life.'

At precisely the same time a church in the Potteries was celebrating its grant of £84,000 from the National Heritage Fund which would be used for the second phase of their building restoration programme. The church is a Grade 2 listed building and a spokesman for it, Gordon Baynham, said there had been 'no adverse reactions just astonishment at how well we've done.'

Individual Christians seem equally confused. Two letters appeared in the *Cambridge Evening News* in that same week of October 1995 – both from Christians. One said: 'The National Lottery is an enormous con trick by the Government. Quite cynically the Government is taxing the poor to benefit the rich. They could set limits on the jackpot but they will not risk that in case it kills the goose that lays the golden egg. Many deserving charities are clearly losing out as people spend their money on a flutter or the Lottery instead of donating directly to the charities. Some may in fact have to shut up shop. Gambling is as much an addiction as alcohol and smoking and nowadays we recognise some people need help to avoid getting hooked. Yet with the Lottery the Government is positively encouraging us to spend, spend, spend. When will they assign some of the Lottery profits to Gamblers Anonymous?'

The other said: 'I am a practising Christian but do not agree that the Lottery is a tax on the poor. I am poor myself. I am long-term unemployed and receive £93 a fortnight to live on. I put £1 in the collection each week and spend £1 a week on the Lottery. One Saturday in the summer three of my numbers came up which meant I won £10.'

The widely differing views expressed within the Church must surely indicate the need for more Christian teaching on money issues. Perhaps discussions could take place in house groups on the basis of the following chapter.

CHAPTER 12

A CHRISTIAN PERSPECTIVE

Even throughout church history there have been differing emphases on the problems and rights and wrongs of gambling. In this chapter we will look briefly at some of these views before trying to establish some form of biblical framework to help answer the questions that the Lottery causes Christians to ask. To help us do this we perhaps ought to start with a definition of gambling. It is 'an agreement between two parties whereby the transfer of something of value is made dependent on an uncertain event in such a way that one party will gain and the other lose.' This may include games of skill but the element of chance is the predominant factor. It should be noted therefore that casting lots in the Bible was not gambling – it was done to discover the will of God.

So how does this apply to the Lottery? Well the philosophy of the Lottery is to get rather than to share. The hope of a buyer of a Lottery ticket or scratch card is to get the property of one's neighbour by chance. Somehow fate, luck or chance (which are all non-Christian concepts) will miraculously change our lives and we will live happily ever after. This is a flight from reality and totally unscriptural. Christians are told to 'put their hope in God who provides richly for our enjoyment' (1 Tim 6:17) and therefore rather than be looking for a lucky break we can face life in the full confidence of God's love and care for us, knowing that he will give us the strength to face whatever comes.

Therefore as Christians we have a choice to make. We cannot serve both God and money (Matthew 6:25). That is why Tertullian said, 'If you say you are a Christian when you are a dice player, you say what you are not for you are a partner with the world.' Jeremy Taylor in his sermon on cards (1660) asked 'If a man be willing or indifferent to lose his own money and not at all desirous to get another's to what purpose is it that he plays for it? If he is not indifferent then he is covetous or a fool, he covets that which is not his own or unreasonably ventures that which is.'

William Temple gave four reasons why he believed gambling is wrong:

1. It glorifies chance not God (1 Cor 14:33).
2. It disregards the stewardship principle (see later).
3. Profit by gambling depends on someone else's loss. Where is love for our neighbour?
4. Those who promote it depend for their appeal to human covetousness. Where is the denial of self? (Exodus 20:17, Luke 12:15).

Thomas Aquinas, on the other hand, believed gambling was permissible provided it was not motivated by covetousness.

Bringing things up to date, differing views still remain. The Roman Catholic church, as has already been mentioned, has a more relaxed view of gambling. Dr John Polkinghorne of the Church of England Board for Social Responsibility has said, 'It would only be right not to take the money for good causes if one felt it was morally tainted; like money, for instance, got by fraud. My doubts about the wisdom of the Lottery do not amount to that.' But John Martin, then editor of the *Church of England Newspaper*, took a much stronger line. 'What makes the National Lottery so pernicious is that it offers people a false God. It certainly tempts us to break the tenth commandment "Thou shalt not covet". Even more importantly it invites us to break the first, "Thou shalt have no other gods before me". It invites us to indulge our imaginations on all the attractions of Mammon.'

Martyn Eden, Evangelical Alliance Home and Public Affairs Director, made the point that though it would be easy for Christians opposed to the Lottery simply not to buy tickets, non-involvement is not enough. He stated that there were four issues which Christians should consider closely when thinking about the National Lottery:

1. Britain had one of the largest gambling industries in Europe in terms of spending per head even before the Lottery started. In other words there were more than enough opportunities to gamble already. There was a real danger that the extra money would largely come from people on very low incomes who would be encouraged to bet money they could ill-afford on a microscopic chance of winning a huge sum.

2. In time the Government could well use Lottery money as a substitute for public spending. This is already the case in arts and sports. So what comes next? Rev Brian Duckworth of the Methodist Church has pointed out that the Christian approach is to pay national bills through the tax system and not through a Lottery.

3. The National Lottery may well succeed only at the expense of giving. Already Christian agencies which rely heavily on the support of the general public must be nervous at the prospect of a reduction in their income. For the uncommitted or casual giver the comforting knowledge that some Lottery proceeds will go to charity may incline them to buy a ticket instead.

4. We need to apply biblical teaching. The biblical principle of Christian giving must surely dictate that it be motivated by gratitude to God and not by a sneaking hope that there will be a jackpot pay-off. Scripture may not specifically condemn gambling but several biblical themes can guide our thinking. Hebrew 13:5 and 1 Timothy warn us about the love of money. Moreover the sad plight of those caught in gambling addiction must not be overlooked.

One newspaper in New Zealand had a policy of never featuring National Lottery winners until one year after their windfall. All too often the stories were sad, with reports of marriage break-down and other tragedies brought on by the fact that people were unable to cope with their new found wealth. Christians are not killjoys but Scripture's guidelines bring about common sense living.

The general weakness of the Church's position was highlighted in an article by Nick Gordon in *The Independent* in April 1995. In it he wrote 'Everything is short-term, so what the hell let's gamble, because gambling is a way of reaching heaven without having to go through the process of dying. In this country the last great strike against gambling came as far back as 1825 when the last state lottery in this country was abolished through the efforts of the anti-slave trade reformer William Wilberforce. That was at a time when the Church sought to protect society from perceived evils. Today the Church is part of the gambling world – it speculated on the property market and lost; its opposition to this summer's introduction of Sunday betting shop opening was feeble. In the absence of a Wilberforce perhaps every race card, betting slip, gaming table, slot machine, share certificate, pools form and lottery ticket in the country should have printed on it a government health warning…an appropriate wording might be "Gambling damages the soul, the intellect and the pocket."'

Biblical principles

Good stewardship
As Christians we are called to be responsible in the way we handle 'our' money. If we accept that God is master and we are stewards then we must transfer ownership of all our possessions to God. 'Any of you who does not give up everything he has cannot be my disciple' (Luke 14:33). There is also a strong warning about the need to handle money God's way later on in Luke. 'Whoever can be trusted with very little can

also be trusted with much and whoever is dishonest with very little will also be dishonest with much. So if you have not been trustworthy in handling worldly wealth who will trust you with true riches' (Luke 16:10-12). This raises awkward questions for us, particularly if we are thinking of buying a Lottery ticket. These include:

• Am I being trustworthy with the money God has given me?
• How do I spend money?
• Do I ever waste money?
• To whom and how much should I give?
• Would Jesus have the same priorities as I do?

Concern for our weaker neighbour

Many people can probably 'afford' to lose the odd pound or two on a Lottery ticket without it doing them too much damage. But this does not mean it is right to do so. 1 John 2:10 says, 'Whoever loves his brother lives in the light and there is nothing in him to make him stumble.' There are many people who are struggling to make ends meet. When we waste money on buying Lottery tickets we are in effect saying we would rather throw our money away than use it to help meet the needs of our brother or neighbour.

This principle of restricting one's legitimate freedom to discourage another from participating in some potentially harmful activity recurs throughout the New Testament. For example, we read in Romans 15:1-2, 'We who are strong ought to bear with the failings of the weak and not to please ourselves. Each of us should please his neighbour for his good, to build him up.' Christians may well consider this to be personally applicable in the case of the Lottery but surely it should also apply to Government policy. Few would wish to argue that people should not have the freedom to gamble but that does not mean that it needs prioritising by the Government. As more people become impoverished, addicted to gambling and more families destroyed the Government cannot evade responsibility and simply say it is down to the individual whether he chooses to gamble.

Responsibility for dependants
In so far as buying Lottery tickets or scratch cards reduces the ability to look after the immediate family and dependants it is biblically unacceptable. 'If anyone does not provide for his relatives and especially for his immediate family, he has denied the faith and is worse than an unbeliever' (1 Tim 5:8).

Poor witness
We are called to be 'lights that shine on a hill'. Buying Lottery tickets can cause bad testimony but also may make us feel guilty and thus be less willing to profess our Christian faith. We are in the world but not of it.

Productive work
Work is both an important means of personal satisfaction and also useful for gaining wealth. By introducing a chance ideology we are in danger of destroying the work ethic found throughout the Bible.

Generosity
Paul encouraged the Corinthian church, 'Just as you excel in everything...see that you excel in this grace of giving' (2 Cor 8:7). Later on in verse 12 Paul is anxious to stress that it is the benevolent nature that is of greatest value, 'If the willingness is there the gift is acceptable according to what one has, not according to what he does not have.' Jesus' comments on seeing the widow putting the mite into the offering box confirm that God does not look at what we give to him but he does look at what we keep for ourselves and how we use it. It is vital to remember too that much which could so easily come under the state's social welfare umbrella is currently being funded by people giving freely of their money and their services. The Government could not fulfil its aims without this high degree of philanthropy. It is therefore not just for the individual good to give with no hope of reward, for the country it is economically essential.

Rest and recreation

As a slight counterbalance to the argument it must be pointed out that the Bible clearly says that rest and recreation are of value. It could be argued that the National Lottery plays its part in this. It has become a major area of communication and has encouraged healthy social interaction in families and in the workplace. There have to be some positive benefits to this.

Contentment

Many Christians should perhaps see that gambling is a sign of dissatisfaction with their lot. Hebrews 13:5 tell us, 'Keep your lives free from the love of money and be content with what you have.' The word 'contentment' appears seven times in the Bible and six times it is in relation to money. Paul also clearly tells us that contentment is something we have to learn, we are not born with it. Contentment is not the same as fatalistic inactivity, still less should it engender a callous attitude to those who have less than we do.

By placing the possibility, however remote, of enormous winnings within the apparent grasp of people it actually means that the Government is increasing the 'feel bad' factor. And discontent with one's present lot – be it home, job, income or whatever – far from promoting harder work actually encourages consumer debt which then becomes harder and harder for people to get out of. We have been warned! 'Godliness with contentment is great gain. For we brought nothing into the world and we can take nothing out of it, but if we have food and clothing we will be content with that. People who want to get rich fall into temptation and a trap and into many foolish and harmful desires that plunge them into ruin and destruction. For the love of money is the root of all kinds of evil. Some people, eager for money, have wandered from the faith and pierced themselves with many griefs' (1 Tim 6:6-14).

Storing up treasures

The key question for all Christians is, where do we want to store up treasures? The Bible makes it very clear that we have to choose; there is no place for compromise. 'Do not store up for yourselves treasures on earth where moth and rust destroy and where thieves break in and steal. But store up for yourselves treasure in Heaven where moth and rust do not destroy and where thieves do not break in and steal. For where your treasure is there your heart is also... No one can serve two masters. You cannot serve both God and money' (Matthew 6:19-21, 24-25).

Money and the desire for riches are likely to be the major drawbacks in our relationships with Christ. The dangers of this are clear. Mark's gospel tells us that it is easier for a camel to go through the eye of a needle than for a rich man to enter the Kingdom of God – and in worldwide terms almost all of us in the West are rich! All of us need to be aware of just how harmful gambling can be. We need to heed the warnings in Ezekiel 7:19: 'Their silver and their gold will not be able to save them in the day of the Lord's wrath. They will not satisfy their hunger or fill their stomachs with it for it has made them stumble into sin.'

Nowhere is this more clearly summed up than in what is sometimes misleadingly called the Parable of the Unjust Steward found in Luke 16. Four points are clearly defined in this parable:

1   (Verse 8) If only believers were as keen to reach the Kingdom as the unbeliever is in making money then things would be very different.

2   (Verse 9) Money may not buy love but it certainly can buy friends. The Jewish belief was that charity should be given to the poor in order to gain credit for themselves in the world to come. Wealth was thus measured by what you gave away not by what you kept for yourself.

3   (Verses 10 and 11) Do well in small tasks and you will be given the opportunity for greater things, i.e. in heaven you will be rewarded according to your life on earth.

4   (Verse 13) No one can serve two masters – serving God is a full-time occupation.

What this story is telling us is that how we handle our money now can affect all eternity. It is about real faith and real commitment to Christ and his values. I can think of no better way of finishing this chapter than asking you to ponder the following quote from John White's book *Money isn't God – so why are we worshipping it?*

'It is want of faith that makes us opt for earthly rather than heavenly treasure. If we *really* believed in celestial treasures who amongst us would be so stupid as to buy gold? We just do not believe. If people believed in heaven they would spend all their times preparing for permanent residence there but nobody does.'

Therefore, as Christians, we need to examine both our attitudes and our actions closely and listen to what God says about the Lottery – even if we don't really like what he has to say.

CHAPTER 13

WHERE DO WE GO FROM HERE?

A s I mentioned earlier, when the Lottery was launched in a blaze of publicity nearly everybody seemed to be in favour, apart from a few Christians and church groups who were regarded as killjoys. As I write this just over a year later there are real signs that some sectors of public opinion are turning against it. In December 1995 there was a *Panorama* special about the National Lottery. The review of the programme in the *Daily Mail* said, 'The Lottery has made 150 millionaires and raised millions for good causes but while Camelot makes large profits *Panorama* asks whether the company is the real winner in the game that has gripped the nation.' It was in this programme that Richard Branson made allegations that Guy Snowden (the co-founder of G-Tech) had attempted to bribe him to pull out of the lottery bidding. He also said that he had warned Peter Davis, the Oflot Director General, of this but Mr Davis had no such recollection. Nevertheless, following consultation with the Department of National Heritage, Mr Davis announced an enquiry into the whole affair and stated that he was appointing a 'senior and independent figure to conduct an investigation into these allegations'...'It is my duty to ensure those involved in the operation of the National Lottery are fit and proper to do so and it is to this question that the investigation will be directed.' A couple of days later

Ann Rafferty QC, Chairman of the Criminal Bar Association, was appointed to this role.

In the same issue there was a two-page article about the biggest single winner of the jackpot which took place exactly a year ago. The article partly indicates why we make our first recommendation for the benefit of individuals.

Recommendation 1   No roll-over jackpot

It is quite clear that when no jackpot is won and the prize is rolled over the following week that ticket sales increase by 20% or more. Many of these tickets are being bought by the same people, who are simply buying more. Of these quite a considerable number will, in the desperation of 'needing' to win, be spending money that they cannot afford and many will also be borrowing money or failing to buy essentials. But research also shows that roll-over jackpot prizes can cause desperation for the winners as well. The *Daily Mail* article began by saying, 'The astonishing jackpot of £17.8 million should have bought joy and lifelong security for the family that won. Instead it has led to a living nightmare which has torn husband from wife and relative from relative in their large extended family. Money has in fact bought them everything except happiness. According to the tabloid press, which can of course be prone to exaggerate, during their turbulent year:

- They argued as to whether to go public and talk to the newspapers about their win.
- They haggled over spending money in London because things were so expensive.
- They moved away from their first holiday hotel because it was too expensive and they felt they didn't fit in.
- Publicity meant they were followed around the world.
- The husband turned to drinking on his own at night.
- His wife was upset by her husband's drinking and was missing their home town.

- The man's brother argued with him saying they should have had more of the money than his wife. They suggested he divorce her.
- After a series of 'accidents' in their home the police were called in.
- The money was held only in the husband's name so the wife made the children wards of court to prevent him taking them away.
- The wife started legal action to ensure she had a right to half the money so her husband conceded with a joint account but with every cheque needing both signatures.
- The wife was not allowed to buy anything without her husband knowing exactly what it was.
- They lived a life of 'tit-for-tat' so if one bought an expensive car then so did the other.
- There was so much bitterness that the money was not invested. This incurred a tax bill of £400,000 and missed investment income of up to £1.5 million.
- They have had legal costs of over £250,000.
- The wife and children disappeared in May because the pressure was too intense.
- The husband and his brothers tried to extract the whereabouts of his wife from her brother which resulted in them being detained until the police were satisfied that the family were safe.
- A friend threatened to sue for a share of the winnings.
- The man was ostracised by both former workmates and fellow Muslims who criticised his gambling.
- The man is suing his wife's brother because he alleges he forged a cheque for £100,000.
- A pre-divorce settlement has been established between the couple.

(Information from *Daily Mail*, 11 December 1995, *Sunday Times*, 16 April 1995, and others.)

Big roll-overs lead people deeper into debt and increase the likelihood of more people becoming compulsive gamblers.

They don't seem to do much good for the winners either if the sorry tale above is in any way typical.

Recommendation 2   Cap jackpot payouts
For reasons already given we would also recommend the capping of jackpot payouts. The first prize could still be at a very attractive level (say £1.5 million). This would mean, first, there would be more big winners, secondly, the sums would be more manageable for the winners and, thirdly, the promise of mega-millions of pounds, however remote the likelihood of success, would be removed.

At the inquest of the suicide victim who thought he had missed out on millions by failing to renew his ticket numbers the coroner said that a smaller jackpot would not impose such a huge pressure. The Rt Rev David Sheppard, Anglican Bishop of Liverpool, has also said that the size of the payouts were out of proportion and led people to become obsessive about winning. This was clearly seen in January 1996 when the double roll-over led to a jackpot of £42 million and people bought many more tickets than usual. There were reports of overseas syndicates operating and of individuals spending up to £10,000.*

Recommendation 3   Increase the minimum age to eighteen
Given the number of press reports and actual surveys undertaken which show a significant number of children under the age of sixteen buying Lottery tickets and scratch cards illegally, the minimum age of purchase should be moved to eighteen in line with other forms of gambling. Because the popularity is partly induced by the television programme it is also suggested that:

- the television programme is moved until after 9 o'clock.

- features such as 'Mystic Meg' are removed from the programme. Even though many will see predictions of win-

Despite these real fears there are indications that Camelot are planning to introduce a superdraw guaranteeing a top prize of approximately £20 million.

ners in a game made up totally of chance as facile there will be other, more gullible, people likely to begin to take in values based on luck/prediction/stars, etc. These are not the values we need to teach our children, nor should we be teaching them that we can increase our chances of winning by buying lottery pens, charms or computer programmes. These gimmicks benefit only the people who manufacture them and sell them at large profits to the naive.

Recommendation 4   Carry out detailed research to discover the extent of the gambling problem

As a result of gambling people can lose their jobs, marriages can break down and, because it is an addiction, it can lead people to steal, borrow more than they can afford to or sell everything they have to acquire the necessary stake money. The Mintel survey found that 17% of regular participants had taken up gambling since the commencement of the National Lottery. If gambling was not a problem then Gamblers Anonymous would not exist.

It is therefore recommended that the Government should set up a Gambling Research Unit which could be funded by the tax the State takes on the ticket sales, the profits of Camelot by special 'windfall' tax or a combination of both. If the Lottery is nothing but 'harmless fun' there is of course nothing to fear. The research should focus on the following:

- Exactly who is buying the Lottery tickets and scratch cards so that 'at risk' groups can be identified. Therefore figures would need to be shown separately for socio-economic groupings, age, gender, income, geographical area, those on benefits, etc.

- The 'at risk' groups should then be studied and monitored over a period of time to compare with 'normal' groups as well as looking for any signs of deterioration in the situation.

- Interviews should take place with representatives of agencies that are directly affected by those who gamble excessively. These would obviously include Gamblers Anonymous, the Samaritans, Relate, money advice and debt counselling agencies, Citizens Advice Bureaux, the churches and the courts.

- As a result of this research conclusions will be reached and in so far as problems become identified actions will need to be taken to alleviate them. These may include both preventative and curative methods.

Preventative

- If research shows that compulsive gambling and the purchase of Lottery tickets and scratch cards are connected then there would need to be an official health warning on the tickets. The warning would need to be worded along the following lines:

    'Beware. Research has shown that some people who buy lottery tickets and scratch cards can get addicted to gambling. Do not spend more than you can afford to lose.'

- Advertising should be more restrained. The amount of money Camelot spends on advertising should be restricted as should the times when it can advertise on television and the places where it can do so. The advertisements should also be more realistic rather than focusing on the 'It could be you' theme.

- The odds should be stated. Both in the advertising and in all places where tickets and scratch cards can be bought posters should be prominently displayed stating the odds of winning the various prizes. This will surely help people prioritise their spending and would be similar to the rules about displaying the Annual Percentage Rate of interest and total costs when buying something using credit.

- The Government should not be involved in promoting the Lottery. Since even before its launch the Government has been making very positive noises about the National Lottery. Whether this is because they launched it and judge by its popularity that it is a vote-winner or simply because it brings much needed millions of pounds of revenue into the Treasury, I do not know. Nevertheless the Government's stance has given the Lottery 'official' backing. People think that if we are being encouraged to play then it must be right to do so and cannot lead to any harm. There is enough encouragement to buy tickets without extra Government support.

Curative

A percentage of the income from ticket sales should be given to address the problems of gambling. If it is found that the National Lottery has directly contributed to an increase in gambling and social problems it should be fairly easy to calculate how much, in real terms, it has cost. Funding should then be provided on an on-going basis to those organisations who have to try and pick up the pieces of wrecked lives. Even a 1% figure which would come out of the Governments 12% tax take (which incidentally is the highest percentage for a state lottery in Europe) would raise tens of millions of pounds and would bring considerable help to both those supplying support and those needing it.

Changes which need to take place to benefit charities

There does seem to be considerable confusion here with the Government and Camelot constantly trumpeting how much money is going to good causes while some major charities complain that their giving is down significantly. The following recommendations are therefore made:

Recommendation 5   Monitoring of giving by the Lottery
One of the aims of Lottery giving is that there should be a fair distribution of giving regardless of income. There have been many complaints made that in fact the giving is bene-

fiting the better-off. Thus the various boards should monitor their giving and report on the spread by socio-economic groupings, age, ethnic groups, inner cities and suburbs, London and the various regions, etc. Although this will not prevent the arguments as to whether, for example, London should have more or less funding at least an accurate picture will be able to be built up. It would be sensible if the Government, presumably the National Heritage Department, collected this information so that analysis could be done on the giving of the five different bodies as well as the group as a whole.

Part of the problem here is partnership – funding where local authorities or other bodies have to provide the balance of the income before the projects can begin. This works to the disadvantage of the poorer council and can thus prevent applications from the areas that need the funding most. For this reason I would propose that a percentage of income from ticket sales is apportioned to help overcome the problems of poorer local authorities applying for funding.

Again a 1% reduction in the Government tax (which combined with the 1% reduction for aiding organisations which help people with gambling problems would mean that the Government's return dropped to 10%) would release significant sums of money that could be used for projects such as, for example, inner city swimming pools. Not only would such facilities be widely used but I believe the Government would actually receive positive feedback from such a move.

Mrs Bottomley has recently indicated that she would like to see lottery funds used to help develop young sporting and artistic talent so hopefully this recommendation may soon come to pass.

Recommendation 6   Revenue funding should be allowed
At the moment all grants made have to be for capital projects. Richer boroughs can therefore apply for large new areas of interest which will add further prosperity to their area whilst some poorer boroughs may not even be able to keep existing facilities open because of lack of funds. Where

this is the case the various Boards should have the discretion to waive the capital rule if a significant number of people in the lower socio-economic groups would benefit by them doing so. This could be done by putting a percentage of their available 'giving' income into an endowment fund which could then be used for specific revenue projects.

In addition to the above I would also suggest that the following also take place:

- Independent monitoring to look at the level of public giving to charities. As these figures are submitted to the Charities Commission they should be easy to evaluate.

- This monitoring should examine carefully whether any Lottery funding is starting to replace what had previously been State funded.

This would help to quantify the situation with regard to the complaints of charities which argue that their income has declined since the introduction of the Lottery. One would be able to see if this was across the board or whether certain groups of charities had suffered particularly badly. Once any particular grouping was established it could be looked at carefully to identify the causes and hopefully begin to apply remedies.

There have been accusations too, that despite firm assurances to the contrary, the Government has been cutting back in certain areas where Lottery funding has been allocated. Reduced spending levels announced for the Arts, Sports and National Heritage can only increase the suspicion. Monitoring of the facts will either confirm or allay any suspicions.

Even if the results of this monitoring do not confirm substantial reductions in public charitable giving (but I fear very much that they would) I propose the following changes that would benefit charities.

**Recommendation 7   An increase in the percentage of
                        Lottery funds going to charities**

Research has shown that the vast majority of people would rather see money going to charities than to any of the other bodies. Given that these other bodies have received an unexpected injection of several hundreds of millions of pounds it would seem only right to increase the amount that charities receive. This would reduce press, public and charities' criticisms and, at the same time, be very popular.

However, it must be remembered that the vast majority of people who buy Lottery tickets do so to win and that therefore what is also needed are moves that will increase giving. These could include:

- A relaxation of tax arrangements to encourage people to give. As it is, by reducing the level of personal tax in the last budget, the Government has reduced the amounts of money that charities get from covenants/gift aid, etc.

- Tax concessions for charities themselves. These would include reducing National Insurance contributions which charities have to pay for their workforce or a reduced rate of VAT for those charities which have a trading arm.

- A percentage of the winner's income going to the charity of his or her choice.

This last recommendation would, I am sure, add considerable interest to the National Lottery. My proposal is simply that 5% of any jackpot prize of over £500,000 would be deducted from the winnings and passed on to the charity or charities of the winner's choice. I do not feel any winner would begrudge this especially if they knew in advance that this was a condition of a jackpot win – who knows it might even salve a few consciences! In addition it is likely to benefit the most well-known charities who have probably suffered most through the downturn in street collection revenue. Some 'celebrity' television shows already have prizes going to the winner's choice of charity so this is hardly an innovative proposal.

How the National Lottery is run and supervised

Despite the fact that the executives responsible for giving Lottery grants to good causes have salaries totalling £1.4 million, the highest paid are Tim Hornsby, who oversees charities grants, and Jennifer Page, head of the Millennium Commission, both of whom earn £80,000. I believe they are all doing a good job but when you compare their salaries to those of the Camelot Board they seem to be significantly underpaid! Perhaps this is why a significant upward review of their salaries took place in March 1996. Tim Holly, Camelot's chief executive, earned over £300,000 in 1995 and under two further types of bonus payment he could earn approaching £700,000 in the future. I have to say that, notwithstanding their undoubted efficiency, for some time I have concurred with Dr Cunningham's view that 'Camelot is not a normal company; it has a licence to print money and in the next few years its directors, who are running a private enterprise monopoly, will be paid bonuses bringing their salaries to over £500,000. I do not believe this, nor the excessive profits of Camelot as a whole, is the right way to run the nation's Lottery.' Camelot forecast, and the Oflot Regulator, Peter Davis (some may say somewhat naively) believed that they would not be profitable for four years and would need three years to write off their capital investment. As it transpired they were in profit almost immediately and wrote off all their capital costs in the first six months.

**Recommendation 9   I therefore propose that the Lottery
                        should be run on non-profit lines**

There are many cases where a healthy profit is essential to continue a capital expansion programme. The National Lottery does not fit into this category. Profits are currently averaging £1 million a week and as has been said, all major capital spending has already been charged to their accounts. Given that Camelot has the contract to run the Lottery to the year 2001 I would invite them to donate 20% of their post tax profit to the National Lottery Charities Board. This would put the company in a better light and also benefit charities without the imposition of a windfall tax which, of course, could be imposed at a higher level, should they not want to donate voluntarily. Another way round this would be to allow Camelot to continue but on a fee-only basis. This could be calculated on the profits they estimated they would make at the time of their submission to run the Lottery.

**Recommendation 10   I believe that the regulatory authority,
                        Oflot, needs significant strengthening**

I have always thought it strange how the regulatory powers to examine things like water, electricity and the Lottery are in the hands of one person. Surely this is too much power for one person to hold and when faced with the fire power of multi-million pound companies they are unlikely to be able to stand up to such pressure. Oflot's job is to 'maximise funds to the good causes' – but by allowing the current levels of profitability, which I regard as excessive, it could be said that they are not doing their job properly. Oflot also too easily accepted Camelot's own assessment that they would make no profit for four years even based on an expected turnover of £100 million a week. Perhaps if the Oflot office had talked to analysts specialising in the leisure sector in any city institution they might have received some help with their sums – expectations there were of a very good and very quick return. As it is, returns on shareholder funds are currently running at around 50% – up to five times higher than average for a leisure company.

The recent allegations about G-Tech, one of the five partners of Camelot, and the way they have been accused of allegedly using underhand and even illegal methods of securing Lottery business only adds to the requirement that Oflot itself is strengthened.

It is quite clear that Mr Davis was badly damaged by the confirmation, in December 1995, that he had used a G-Tech jet to travel around America. His reason that it was 'extremely economical' was not regarded as dishonest but was generally considered very naive. For several days he looked as if he could lose his job but he refused to resign and eventually he was backed by Mrs Bottomley even though she told him that his decision to accept flights from G-Tech had 'not been wise'. There was some debate at the time about whether Mrs Bottomley had the authority to sack him but in any case the meeting between them was 'cordial'.

People are perhaps dissatisfied with his performance for reasons other than accepting free flights or being an old friend of a G-Tech director. I believe that many are not convinced that he has been sufficiently robust and it may be that it is simply too much responsibility for one man. I therefore propose that:

- Oflot's brief must be altered. At present trying to regulate the Lottery whilst at the same time aiming to maximise its income is a clear conflict of interest. It should have a purely regulatory role – there are enough people involved in maximising income already!

- Oflot should be more pro-active in looking at the excess profits Camelot have made over forecast (even if they are completely legal).

- Oflot needs to be accountable to someone to prevent the recurrence of such unfortunate events as Mr Davis suffered in December 1995. A good regulator needs to protect the interests of the individual – as tax-payer, consumer, voter and member of society. He therefore needs the power to regulate effectively which can only be done with full access to management accounts and senior personnel. He should also have the power to withdraw licences where necessary.

Conclusion

Rather like the first jackpot winner who has found it hard to cope, so now the Lottery organisers are being put under increased pressure for more accountability and more clarity in the way in which they operate. They have done a very good job in getting the Lottery up and running on time but they are increasingly looking like a company concerned only with profit and with little concern for the people who buy the tickets or for the 'good causes' who should be benefiting from the Lottery. Perhaps a good public relations exercise is needed here.

But individuals too need to be mindful of the facts about the National Lottery. The odds against winning are astronomical and for the very few who have won it has not brought unconditional happiness. For many £1 a week is 'harmless fun' and also a cheap way of dreaming about those rum punches in the sand and sun of Barbados. For others the drabness of their life around them will be encouraging overspending that could have serious financial and emotional consequences later on.

Many people too are unhappy about where the Lottery money has been given. They are not the good causes they would have chosen. Can I simply say to you, if you want to play the Lottery do so without reference to the giving side. You are playing because you hope to win. But win or lose please do not forget the areas that you want to give to. So if you want to support the Arts keep going to your local theatre and cinema, support sport by going along to see your local football or rugby team or join a swimming or tennis club. And please, please, please continue to support the charities you care about as tax-efficiently as you can. They cannot rely on Lottery funding but they do rely on your on-going support.

In just over a year the National Lottery has permeated our society. It is talked about more than the weather and we frequently hear comments such as 'I'd have to win the Lottery before I could afford that.'

The Lottery is not going to go away but both as individuals and as a society we need to be aware of what it is saying to us and about us. It can undermine benevolence and contentment and promote chance rather than the work ethic. As a Christian, I believe that Jesus taught us to love people and use our money to help others less fortunate than ourselves. For the most part I have to conclude that the National Lottery teaches us to do the reverse.